COACHING
LIFE-CHANGING
small group
LEADERS

Books in the Groups That Grow Series

Building a Life-Changing Small Group Ministry

Coaching Life-Changing Small Group Leaders

Leading Life-Changing Small Groups

Equipping Life-Changing Leaders (DVD)

**A Comprehensive Guide for
Developing Leaders of Groups and Teams**

COACHING

LIFE-CHANGING

small group

LEADERS

BILL DONAHUE AND
GREG BOWMAN

ZONDERVAN.com/
AUTHORTRACKER
follow your favorite authors

ZONDERVAN

Coaching Life-Changing Small Group Leaders
Copyright © 2006, 2012 by Bill Donahue, Greg Bowman, and Willow Creek Association

This title is also available as a Zondervan ebook.

Requests for information should be addressed to:

Zondervan, *Grand Rapids, Michigan 49530*

Library of Congress Cataloging-in-Publication Data

Donahue, Bill, 1958-
    Coaching life-changing small group leaders : a comprehensive guide for developing leaders of
groups and teams / Bill Donahue and Greg Bowman.
       p. cm.—(Groups that grow series)
    ISBN 978-0-310-33124-7 (softcover)
    1. Christian leadership. 2. Small groups—Religious aspects—Christianity. 3. Church group
work. 4. Personal coaching. I. Bowman, Greg, 1960- II. Title.
BV652.1.D66 2012
253'.7—dc23
                                       2011050013

Cover design: Kirk DouPonce
Interior design: Sherri L. Hoffman

Printed in the United States of America

---

12 13 14 15 16 17 /DCI/ 27 26 25 24 23 22 21 20 19 18 17 16 15 14 13 12 11 10 9 8 7 6 5 4 3 2 1

CONTENTS

ACKNOWLEDGMENTS

This is the second edition of *Coaching Life-Changing Small Group Leaders*, evidence that this resource has struck a chord with leaders who need practical tools to help small group leaders lead well. This book would not have had anywhere near the impact it has without the support, contributions, feedback, and wisdom of many other people.

We are indebted to Paul Engle and the Zondervan publishing team, without whom this work would not be in your hands. You have broadened the scope of our ministry and introduced us to many global leaders and group-life zealots. We have enjoyed working with John Raymond, Ryan Pazdur, Brian Phipps, and their teams, who edited and guided the work, and are grateful for the marketing expertise of Mark Kemink and his team.

Thanks also to the C2 Group and the fine work of Mike Seaton and his talented video crew, who brought the vision for the DVD material to life.

We are grateful to all who partnered with us at Willow Creek in earlier days, helping develop and craft the vision and strategy for coaching leaders. The coaches we have worked with over the years have put this material into practice, ensuring that it works and helps guide small group leaders toward excellence and fruitfulness. Without them, this would simply be a book of theories.

In addition, we are so thankful for partner and creative genius Dave Treat, who made contributions to this work. More important, he has real experience training leaders and building group life in several churches. He helped design conferences and events for leaders worldwide with us at the Willow Creek Association (WCA).

The WCA Group Life Team worked for ten years to extend what we were learning about group life to the world. They provided a platform for our vision and ministry, and without them we'd be talking to a handful of people in a church basement. This team includes Wendy Seidman, Stephanie Oakley, Stephanie Walsh, April Kimura-Anderson, and the publishing team of Nancy Raney, Christine Anderson, and Doug Yonamine, and Bill's very capable assistants Joan Oboyski and Cindy Martucci.

Pam Howell and Sherri Meyer brought the best of their skills in arts and production to help the WCA produce a top-notch Group Life Conference for eleven years. This platform allowed us to share ideas, envision future leaders, and encourage group life pastors around the world.

Finally, we are grateful to Bill Hybels and Jim Mellado, who provided the opportunity for us to help lead and shape the group life movement at the WCA and church for many good years.

INTRODUCTION

Welcome to the ministry of coaching! It truly is one of the most satisfying forms of service in the church, a place where you will see your ministry efforts multiplied through the leaders and groups you serve.

If you enjoy doing ministry *through* others, not just *to* others, you'll enjoy coaching.

If you enjoy developing leaders, you'll find coaching to be very rewarding.

If you enjoy having a role in church leadership that interfaces with staff as well as with volunteers, you'll find coaching to be challenging and productive.

And if you want to grow in your personal leadership and in your relationship with Christ, you'll be glad that you are coaching, because it's a catalytic environment for transformation.

THE COACHING MANUAL

This manual is filled with practical ministry ideas, leadership guidance, and strategic exercises to make your coaching ministry a success. It is organized into four chapters.

1. *"A Vision for Coaching."* Here you will understand what a coach is and why the art and ministry of leadership coaching is so essential to the church. Coaching is not a new practice. It might have been called various things throughout the history of God's people, but the practice of one leader coaching other leaders is as old as the Bible.

2. *"Coaching's Core Practices."* Every line of work and every area of expertise has core practices that a person must master if he or she is to be effective in that work. Coaching is no different. Here you will learn to approach coaching using the three major practices of a strategy described as "3-D coaching"—*discover*, *develop*, and *dream*.

3. *"The Coach's Toolbox."* Now that you know what a coach does and the essential practices that shape your work, you need a variety of tools

and resources to carry out the ministry. Here you will learn how to engage in coaching conversations with group leaders, how to foster learning and community among leaders through core gatherings, and how to connect with the small groups in your care. In this chapter, we've provided many ready-to-use implements so you don't have to create everything on your own. We know you have limited time, and we want to maximize your ministry efforts.

4. *"The Coach's Life."* In this chapter, you will learn how to strengthen your spiritual life, manage your schedule, confront stress and burnout, and navigate the demands of work, family, and ministry. We care about you, and so does your church. Most of all, God cares about your long-term role in ministry. Here we focus on ministry sustainability, setting boundaries, creating margin, and engaging in personal spiritual practices that will shape your soul and guard your heart.

DVD MATERIAL

Complementing this resource is a DVD designed for leaders at every level of group ministry, called *Equipping Life-Changing Leaders* (sold separately; ISBN: 9780310331276). The video segments it contains will guide you through *Coaching Life-Changing Small Group Leaders* and help you understand the focus of each of its four chapters. The DVD includes focused teaching, engaging dramas, and other creative elements to inspire you and equip you for leadership.

Before working through each chapter of *Coaching Life-Changing Small Group Leaders*, watch the DVD segment for that chapter. Each video is approximately eight to ten minutes long. Once you have viewed the DVD, you can work through that section of the material at your own pace, or with a group of leaders in your ministry. In many cases, your church leadership will be guiding the process.

It's best to have a partner or other coaches with you so you can encourage one another and share ideas as you work through the material. Perhaps your church leaders have already created some training sessions or classes for coaches. Perhaps there is a chance to meet one-on-one with a staff member or seasoned volunteer leader who can provide guidance, accountability, and a connection to the broader church vision as you learn this role.

However you work through the material, allow yourself time to process what you are reading and to put a plan together for coaching your leaders with excellence, a commitment to Christ, and a heart for people. (We'll show you how to do this.)

We are privileged to serve you in this way, and we hope this material will provide you with the motivation, skills, information, and tools to be a great coach!

Chapter 1

A VISION FOR COACHING

What does it mean to be a coach? Why is it so essential to have people in the church who are willing to guide and encourage leaders of groups and teams? What does it look like when someone takes on this role and invests in the life of a leader?

To become effective coaches in the church, first we need to embrace a vision for the practice of coaching. It is often a misunderstood role, mistaken by some to mean "boss" or "faultfinder." That's not coaching, at least not when the spiritual growth of leaders and church members is at stake. Coaching is different from mere oversight or supervision. It is personal, developmental, and supportive. Coaches bring out the best in leaders. Let's take a few moments to get a clearer picture of what it means to coach leaders in the church.

EVERYONE HAS A STORY

Every coach has a story. Every leader has a story. Each one has his or her struggles and successes. Each group, each ministry team, has a beginning. It has, or soon enough will have, its share of problems, relational challenges, victories and breakthroughs. And at some point, everyone's leadership of his or her group, or the group itself, will come to an end.

What will make the difference in a leader's story? Each day, leaders write a page in their leadership narrative. Every aspect of life is a part of their unfolding story: every decision they face, every conversation they have, every prayer they offer, every relationship they forge, every gathering they participate in, every new skill they learn and practice, every way they try to balance their personal time with their leadership responsibilities. What makes the difference in a leader finding joy and fulfillment as they live out their story?

Woven into the leader's story line are people who offer sage counsel as the story progresses. It's not important that these influencers have all the answers or that their stories are picture perfect. What is important is the willingness to graciously share life in a way that helps other leaders grow. As Proverbs 13:10 tells us, wisdom comes when we listen to each other's counsel.

In many vocations and avocations, this wisdom comes from someone called a coach. This is not a term unique to leaders in our world. Coaches exist everywhere, in every kind of work. Use any search engine on the internet, and you will find millions of sites offering information about the word *coach*.

Executives hire professional coaches to get their businesses running at peak performance and keep their leadership skills sharp. Scan a handful of professional coaching sites, and a few key words and phrases keep popping up: *focus, effectiveness, results, motivation, skill, clarity, time management, follow-through, commitment, cooperation*. Interestingly, coaches for these corporate executives often stress a balance between work and play, business and family.

> Once used to bolster troubled staffers, coaching now is part of the standard leadership development training for elite executives and talented up-and-comers at IBM, Motorola, J.P. Morgan, Chase, and Hewlett Packard. These companies are discreetly giving their best prospects what star athletes have long had: a trusted adviser to help them reach their goals.
>
> — *CNN.com*

John Russell, managing director of Harley-Davidson Europe, Ltd., is an avid fan of coaching because of its ability to bring out the best in leaders. He says, "I never cease to be amazed at the power of the coaching process to draw out the skills or talent that was previously hidden within an individual, and which invariably finds a way to solve a problem previously thought unsolvable."

Life coaches are quick to emphasize they are not therapists; they are more than a friend and more than a consultant. Life coaches are there to help you be successful — to clarify your goals and help you take action. They are there to help you do whatever it takes: eliminate the distractions that suck time, energy, and money from life, upgrade your friends (getting interested?), smooth out your life wrinkles, and create a life plan that works. (Honestly, these words were taken from real websites!) Good life coaches will, in fact, challenge your thinking. They will help you alter ingrained behavior patterns. They can help you make real and lasting changes.

The world of creative arts has long adhered to a coaching model in many disciplines. Dance, drama, sculpting, painting — the list is endless. Coaches are also coming forward to help artists build their business; some are calling it "left-brained skills for right-brained people." These coaches are wise in the way they are tailoring their counsel to the natural ways that artists think and process their world, and the best coaches are helping them bring their artistic discipline to the business of art.

Even in the construction trades (carpentry, electrical work, plumbing), there is a coaching relationship between skilled workers and their apprentices. There are skills to be learned, tools and techniques to be mastered, a language to be understood, relationships and deadlines to be managed. The apprentice takes cues and counsel from the tradesman, his or her coach, who in this case has years of on-the-job experience.

Last, and most obviously, is the world of sports. The list of legendary coaches is topped by names like John Wooden, the UCLA coach whose record of ten NCAA national championships in a twelve-year period is unmatched by any other college basketball coach. Or Pat Summit, who in her four decades as coach of women's basketball at the University of Tennessee has changed the way women's hoops is viewed. Vince Lombardi led his Green Bay Packers football team to five NFL championships in the 1960s. Butch Harmon, the top swing coach for ten years running in the world of golf, has helped shape the game of professionals like Phil Mickelson, Tiger Woods, Ernie Els, and Greg Norman.

Sports coaches help athletes do their best, stay grounded in the fundamentals, never get complacent, overcome the little mistakes that lead to big errors, and always give their all. The best coaches will also help their players with integrity on and off the playing field. It doesn't take long to come up with a list of athletes whose promising careers have been cut short by failings that had little to do with their athletic prowess or performance. As John Wooden said, the challenge is always to give that coaching without causing resentment.

Even the best leaders need a coach, whether they are the top athletes in their chosen sport or successful executives in a large corporation. Leaders need someone to offer a gentle course correction when they stray from the fundamentals. They need a safe environment to process the challenges of leadership, to celebrate the victories, and to determine what actions to take next. Every leader needs a coach who can step into his or her story and bring clarity when the plotline gets confusing, when the narrative is heavy or troubling or involves something the leader has never faced before.

Every leader has a story, and woven into that story are a number of coaches, individuals who have had a positive influence in the leader's growth and development over time.

Take a few minutes and think through your leadership story. What individuals have offered sage counsel to you at various points in your journey? If it is helpful, break your story into ten-year periods of life and single out one or two people who were most influential in a coaching role in each of those periods.

What was it about each coach's relationship and interaction with you that was most helpful?

GOD'S STORY

The Bible is full of stories that describe what happens when a coach or mentor speaks into the life of an ordinary person, investing in an individual who shows leadership potential.

Moses with Joshua

According to Numbers 11, Joshua was one of several men who served as aides to Moses, and Joshua did so from an early point in his life. Moses evidently spotted some leadership potential in him, because over time Joshua was given increasing amounts of leadership responsibility and opportunity.

By the time we encounter Joshua and Moses in the book of Exodus, Joshua has been elevated to the level of a personal assistant to Moses. He experiences lots of up close and personal interaction with Moses. He observes Moses as he leads the nation of Israel spiritually and militarily. Those opportunities contain many great coaching moments.

Moses develops Joshua spiritually by exposing him to incredible experiences with God, like ascending Mount Sinai with Moses to receive the Ten Commandments (Ex. 24). Moses takes Joshua with him into the tabernacle whenever God speaks directly to him (Ex. 33). Moses also takes the opportunity to develop Joshua militarily by asking him to lead the nation into battle (Ex. 17).

Moses coaches Joshua's leadership decision making all along the way. In Numbers 11:27–29, at God's direction, Moses is choosing seventy elders and leaders for Israel. As Moses is talking to the nation, God breaks in and begins speaking as a sign of affirmation for Moses's choices. As God speaks, his Spirit falls on the seventy men, and all of them—including Eldad and Medad, who aren't at the tabernacle with Moses and the others—begin to prophesy.

Joshua expresses a fair amount of jealousy and anger that these two men might be taking Moses's position of leadership. It's understandable that Joshua has grown close to his coach and mentor, but his actions are clearly out of line. Moses corrects Joshua's attitude and teaches him a valuable leadership lesson.

Through Moses's careful coaching, Joshua grows from a timid young man into a man of strong character and strong faith, strong enough that he becomes one of two leaders who profess a belief that Israel can conquer the Promised Land. Joshua takes on partial leadership of Israel (Num. 27:18–23) and eventually, at Moses's death, becomes the sole spiritual and military leader of the nation (Josh. 1:1–9).

Jesus with Peter

The public opinion on Peter was less than kind. One religious group referred to him as "uneducated and inexperienced" (Acts 4:13 CEV). Yet Jesus saw enough potential in Peter to make him one of the first disciples called to join his ministry (Matt. 4:18–20). Peter had leadership gifts and abilities; he just needed a coach who believed in him, a coach who would invest in him and help him grow into the leader God had already gifted him to be.

Over the next three and a half years, Jesus coached Peter's development by

- encouraging Peter to take risks and step out in faith, even when others were afraid to follow (Matt. 14:25–31);

- allowing Peter to speak his opinions but correcting his thinking when he was off base (Matt. 16:22–23);
- exposing Peter to experiences that would stretch his faith as well as his understanding of God's calling on his life (Luke 8:40–56; 9:28–36);
- recognizing when Peter was open to deeper teaching, and directly answering his questions (Matt. 15:15–20; 18:21–35);
- speaking hard truth to Peter when necessary (Matt. 26:34);
- giving Peter specific tasks that would develop his leadership gifts and abilities (Luke 9:1–2; 22:8).

Few leaders have failed Christ as badly as Peter. He denied his friend and teacher three times in his hour of greatest need. Yet Peter rose past his failures and became the rock-solid foundation of the early church. Peter was able to rise above his mistakes, his deficiencies in education, and people's lack of faith in him. He was able to overcome all those obstacles because of the nurture and development he received in his time with Jesus.

Priscilla and Aquila with Apollos

Intimidated by the prospect of coaching people more gifted than you? Take a good look at this New Testament couple. Recruited by Paul in Corinth, Priscilla and Aquila were in the business of tentmaking. When Paul left for Ephesus, they accompanied him in his church-planting ventures. Knowing what we do of Paul, we can easily imagine that the three-hundred-mile journey by boat from Corinth to Ephesus was filled with coaching conversations.

Upon arrival in Ephesus, Paul parted company with this dynamic couple, who apparently felt energized for ministry. Soon they found themselves coaching the great orator Apollos, a superstar communicator who taught some questionable doctrine. Though he could teach circles around them, Priscilla and Aquila guided and coached him, releasing him back into ministry.

What made Pricilla and Aquila the right coaches for Apollos was not superior training, skills, or experience. It was their ability to speak truth to Apollos in such a way that he could receive it and immediately apply it to his life.

An easily overlooked aspect of these stories in Acts 18 is that high-impact coaching can take place in a relatively short time span. Coaches can catalyze growth in leaders in a single interaction. It doesn't always take months or years to make a difference in a leader's life.

Paul with Timothy

If you read the book of Acts through the coaching lens, the apostle Paul stands out for the energy he invested to raise up and develop new leaders.

The list of people he coached includes not only Priscilla and Aquila but also Barnabas, John Mark, Silas, and a young man named Timothy, whom Paul encountered in the city of Lystra.

Timothy had a good reputation with the church there and also in the nearby town of Iconium (Acts 16:2), where he had evidently done some work. Paul saw enough potential in this young leader to take him along on his church-planting travels.

Paul coached Timothy in ways to avoid unnecessary conflict (Acts 16:3) and unnecessary physical danger (Acts 17:13 – 15) and gave him responsibilities that would catalyze growth (Acts 19:22). Paul coached Timothy the same way he coached other young leaders, but over time a special connection developed between these two men.

Paul was especially fond of Timothy. You can hear it in the tone of his writing to and about Timothy. Paul gave the church at Corinth instructions to protect Timothy and take good care of him (1 Cor. 16:10). He told another church that Timothy had earned their trust because he had proven himself (Phil. 2:22).

The longer Paul and Timothy were in this coaching relationship, the closer they became. Paul first described Timothy as "my co-worker" (Rom. 16:21) and "our brother" (Col. 1:1), both generic terms Paul used for several of his ministry partners and mentees. But Paul's descriptions of Timothy progressed to "my son whom I love" in 1 Corinthians 4:17, when Paul wrote about this young teacher he was sending to help the church.

By the time Paul was nearing the end of his life, he wrote a personal letter to Timothy and addressed him as "my true son in the faith" (1 Tim. 1:2). As happens many times, the coaching relationship had gone beyond professional or personal development. A rich, deep bond had been formed. Because of the depth of this bond, Paul was able to offer very direct words to Timothy in regard to

- the direction of Timothy's work (1 Tim. 1:3);
- Timothy's gifting and call from God (1 Tim. 1:18);
- Timothy's personal integrity and spiritual purity (1 Tim. 6:11 – 16, 20);
- the need to follow Paul's example (2 Tim. 3:10).

The rich texture of their relationship allowed Paul to speak into all areas of Timothy's life and development and catalyze deep change. As a result, Timothy became a tremendous leader in the early church. For example, Paul's investment in Timothy enabled him to speak courageously in the church at Ephesus at the height of cultural chaos and doctrinal confusion.

"Clean up this mess, Timothy!" challenged Paul, and Timothy rose to the occasion.

REFLECTION

1. Review the biblical coaching examples above. What stands out as examples of how you would respond best to coaching?

2. What ideas do you glean from these biblical examples that you would like to begin to add to your coaching of other leaders?

CHAD AND ERIC'S STORY

Three years ago Chad discovered Community Church, and he has been fully engaged there ever since. When he first got involved in small group leadership, he had worked with Sean and Allison, a couple who had provided timely wisdom for Chad while he was launching his first group. Though he had only known them for twelve months or so, Chad had grown close to this couple.

Sean and Allison had talked Chad through his challenges as a growing believer. They had helped him think through challenges at work and relationship issues with his girlfriend, Jaclyn.

They had talked about Chad's group too. The conversations they had about the group always made it feel to Chad as if his small group were an integrated part of his life. The coaching relationship felt easy and natural. When Sean and Allison said they were praying for him, Chad got the sense they really meant it.

His small group of twelve was a group of nine just a few months ago. Adding a few new folks has been good for the group, but it has also brought some challenges. To Chad, it feels as if the group is starting over.

Recently Chad was shocked and saddened when he learned that Allison's work would transfer her and her husband, Sean, out of state. Only later did Chad realize that this meant he would be getting a new coach.

A novice at group leadership, Chad is now navigating his relationship with his new coach, Eric. Eric has been coaching for almost five years. He does it because deep in his soul he knows it fits his gifts, passion, and personal vision for ministry. This leadership role allows him to invest himself in the lives of other leaders, fulfilling his ministry and, with God's help, shaping theirs.

Eric is not the kind of coach you would find barking commands from the sidelines of a football field or pacing frantically up and down the basketball court, shouting out plays and correcting players. His ministry is more like the work of a golf or tennis coach, bringing out the best in others by providing them meaningful feedback and supporting them with practical resources.

Currently Eric is guiding a handful of group leaders toward greater ministry success and encouraging them toward deeper personal growth. He loves doing ministry through others — not simply *to* others — and really enjoys watching group leaders flourish.

Eric has just been assigned the responsibility of coaching Chad, and not long ago he left this message on Chad's phone: "Hey, Chad, this is Eric. I shot you an email last week but haven't heard back from you. I'm your new coach in the small group ministry at Community Church. Give me a call when you get a chance. Hope you get this message. Here's my cell phone number ..."

Chad ignored the email and the voicemail message for a few days, reluctant to connect with Eric.

Launching and leading this small group has been the biggest challenge of Chad's spiritual life, and he knows he needs some help. He's just been hesitant to begin a new coaching relationship.

Eric, on the other hand, is struggling to interpret Chad's avoidance. He wrote about this in his journal: "Lord, you know how much I love helping leaders. I realize that the mature leaders in my care need less coaching than Michelle, Stephen, and Chad. But I'm disappointed that Chad seems to be avoiding me. Saw him in church again, but he didn't acknowledge me. I confess I felt awkward, not needed, like maybe this is a relational mismatch. Help Chad understand that I want to get to know him and want to see his life and ministry flourish."

It's now Monday evening, around nine o'clock. Chad has settled down after a long day. His group meets tomorrow evening. He takes a deep breath and grabs his cell phone to call Eric back.

"Eric? Hi, this is Chad returning your call."

"Hey, Chad," Eric replies, relieved to finally make contact with Chad. "It's great to hear from you! I saw you the last couple weeks at church and wondered if I should just come up and say hello or wait for you to get back to me. In case you've been swamped with work, I decided to just leave the ball in your court."

Chad is apologetic, and he wonders how exactly Eric recognized him. He is nervous, hoping that the conversation won't move from uncomfortable to downright awkward.

"Sorry ... I saw your email and also got your message. Just been a little slow getting back to some folks." Chad thinks for a moment. Has he ever met Eric? "I'm not sure I can put a face with your name. But it sounds like we've met before. Obviously, I'm the clueless one here."

Chad feels uncomfortable because he is usually on top of things and rarely forgets a name. His attention to detail and his ability to manage lots of information make him an ideal IT professional. Right now he feels a little out of the loop, and that's an uncomfortable place for him to be.

"We were in Pastor's class on the gospel of Mark two summers ago," says Eric, "and we sat at the same table a couple times."

Eric's words are upbeat and lack any kind of condescension or disappointment.

"I'm impressed. You have a good memory. I'd probably recognize you if I saw you," replies Chad with a hopeful tone.

"Well, now you'll get the chance! How about a cup of coffee later this week or a quick bite to eat after church?"

"I think I can make either work. Let me check my calendar and shoot you an email."

Later that night, Eric writes in his journal again, this time acknowledging his own insecurities: "Okay, God, there I go again. Quick to judge and feeling insecure. How do I expect to keep coaching leaders when I can't seem to get over this character flaw myself? After all these years, I still slip into old patterns. Looks like you're working in Chad despite me. No surprise there. Thanks."

Sitting down at the coffee shop Sunday after church, Eric asks Chad to share his story. "So, tell me about your journey the last few years at Community Church. What brought you here, and how did you get connected into group leadership?"

Chad is relieved. He finds Eric's communication style to be direct and engaging, and it's easy to open up and talk. Eric smiles as he listens, and he doesn't seem to have that hyperspirituality or relational intensity that often makes Chad uncomfortable. He appears to be genuinely interested, a trait Chad admired in his former coaches, Sean and Allison.

"I know we're just getting to know each other," Eric probes, "but I wonder if there's anything about you or the group I could pray for this week."

Their first meeting ends well. As Chad thinks about it, he realizes that Eric didn't even discuss church strategy or small group structure. The entire meeting was all about him, Chad ... and he did most of the talking. Eric simply asked good questions and spent most of his time listening.

REFLECTION

1. Think back through the relationship between Chad and his first coaches, Sean and Allison. What did Chad receive in this relationship that made it so helpful and important to him?

2. What did Eric do to help Chad with the transition to a new coach?

UNPACKING THE STORY

If you have been a leader or a coach for very long, perhaps you can identify with one or more parts of this story.

Perhaps you identified with the joy of the solid coaching relationship Chad enjoyed with Sean and Allison. They were able to speak into more areas of Chad's life than just his small group leadership because they invested time and energy in the relationship. Over time, he shared his spiritual journey with them. As a new leader and a relatively new Christian, Chad was on the ragged edge of adventure. God was teaching him, stretching him, growing him as much as he was using him to help members of the group grow. God often does that when we step into a leadership role.

Chad needed a safe place to process the new challenges and opportunities he was facing; sometimes he needed it more than he realized. Sean and Allison provided a safe environment for him in casual, nonthreatening conversations at the café, at the church, and sometimes through quick messages over the web.

Over time, Chad also began to talk more about his challenges and successes at work. He even began to talk about his dating life with Jaclyn. Chad opened up his heart and began to share on a deeper level with Sean and Allison as trust grew between them. They began to understand more of who Chad was, how God had uniquely gifted him, and what God was up to in his life and in his group.

Beyond investing in their relationship with Chad, Sean and Allison also invested in Chad's leadership ability. Those conversations came later, after the trust and the personal relationship had grown. Chad knew from the beginning that this relationship was about more than three people meeting for coffee and conversation, but Sean and Allison didn't seem to force the issue.

They listened to Chad, really listened, as he talked about the group. They asked great questions about what was going on in the group. And when needs or problems came up, their reaction was great! Because they had been leaders for several years, Sean and Allison didn't act surprised or shocked. In fact, they seemed to *expect* that problems were going to come. They helped Chad think through how best to work through each issue in a loving and Christlike way that helped everyone grow.

All along the way, they helped him find the right resources—people to talk with, books, online material, training, whatever he needed. They didn't always have the answers, but they would work with Chad to find the help he needed for whatever he was facing.

Chad's confidence grew with every challenge he faced. You could sense it in the way he led the group and in the way he cared for the members. He moved beyond those first faltering steps of leadership, those first awkward group meetings. He began to take risks, to ask deeper questions, and to try new approaches to the meetings.

Now, rather than simply meeting together twice a month on Tuesday, the members of the group were enjoying connecting with each other outside of meetings as well as at church gatherings. They had recently taken the bold step of inviting new people to join the group—all as a result of Sean and Allison's gentle and consistent efforts to expand Chad's vision for what God might do in and through his group.

A coach can be one of the most high-impact volunteer leaders in the local church.

- *Coaches can inspire leaders to have a deeper walk with Christ.* The one-to-one, shepherding nature of the relationship often affords the leader the chance to be transparent and vulnerable in a way that is not possible in other settings. Speaking into a leader's walk with God will have the greatest impact on his or her life and leadership.
- *Coaches can draw out untapped potential in leaders.* You may see new spiritual gifts, talents, or abilities that leaders are not aware they possess. When a coach names that potential and walks with a leader as he or she explores it, it's exciting for both of them.
- *Coaches can encourage.* We've all been there or will be soon enough. A bad meeting or two. A tough conflict in the group. People dropping out or moving away. Discouragement comes to the best leaders. Often a simple word of encouragement is the key to a leader staying in the game.
- *Coaches can give permission to rest or risk.* The objective perspective a coach brings can help a leader discern if it's time, personally or for the group, to take a break. Is it rest we need? Or is it a new challenge that will bring fresh vitality?
- *Coaches can give the space and time to listen deeply.* Life-changing coaching will demand that you surrender your most valued possession: unhurried chunks of time—time to hang out with leaders, time to learn their story, process their challenges, and brainstorm solutions. You may in some ways become a shepherd for them. (The word used most often in the Bible is *pastor*, but that carries too much baggage in our culture!)

REFLECTION

As you consider the ministry of coaching, which of these five points reso-
nate most with you? Why?

1. Coaches can inspire leaders to have a deeper walk with Christ.

2. Coaches can draw out untapped potential in leaders.

3. Coaches can encourage.

4. Coaches can give permission to rest or risk.

5. Coaches can give the space and time to listen deeply.

Group leaders—especially new leaders like Chad—are not sure they are being effective when they lead a small community. Developing people is hard work, and the fruit of a leader's labor may not be seen for weeks, months, or even years. The difference between a leader who merely endures and one who enjoys leadership can be made by a coach who walks with a leader to encourage, cast vision, and assure them they are not crazy for investing their time and energy in this "community thing."

If you are truly called and equipped to coach, there is no greater thrill than to help a leader thrive! To have a ringside seat to Chad's growth as a leader, as a Christ follower—what could be more thrilling than that? Perhaps you smiled, felt your heart race a little, as you read about how Sean and Allison were investing in Chad.

In the midst of this successful coaching relationship came the reality of change. Change is never easy, but relational change seems especially hard. It was hard for Chad. He had grown so close to Sean and Allison. He had opened up his heart to them. The early part of his walk as a Christian had been marked with disappointment in the local church. He had developed no friends, he had felt no connection, and he had sensed no real way to make a difference. But all of his hopes had come together after connecting with Sean and Allison.

Maybe you can relate to what Eric went through. Your leaders just aren't responding, in spite of all your prayers and all your efforts to reach out. Eric is a good coach, maybe a great one, but he was handed a tough transition, sort of like an arranged marriage with a jilted spouse. He prays for the leaders in his care, and that's huge! He's been gracious and patient in his pursuit of Chad in this coaching relationship. His journal entries reveal that he's pretty self-aware. The odds are good that Chad's initial fears and apprehension were misplaced. Eric will likely be a wonderful coach for him. But it will take time and work to build a good foundation for their coaching relationship.

LEARNING FROM THE STORY

If you look closely at examples from the professional, personal, and biblical realms, a model for effective, life-changing coaching begins to emerge.

You can see it if you look carefully at Chad's story. Chad could be any of the thousands of leaders we have met, trained, or talked with whose personal journey tells the same story; for each of those leaders, the word *coach* is best understood as a verb, not a noun. Their stories teach us that coaching is more about the actions you take than the title you assume. It's about a relationship, not a reporting structure. It's about encouragement, not management. If any coach ever loses sight of those simple truths, he has lost the heart and the power of coaching.

While it is not uncommon for a coach to develop close friendships with their leaders, the purpose of the relationship goes far beyond that. It goes beyond a cup of coffee, a casual conversation and check-in on life. Coaching can and should include those elements (especially the coffee!), but if the relationship stops there, the coach is missing a key component of the role God is calling them to play in the life of each leader they serve.

For more than thirty years, each of us (Bill and Greg) has recruited, trained, and worked with coaches in the local church. We've been in the trenches, just like you, working with individual leaders of groups and teams. In addition, we have worked with churches in a variety of settings as consultants and trainers. Our experience, which covers a wide range of ministry models, cultures, and denominations, has brought us to crystal clarity on the purpose of coaching. The simplest way we know to say it is this:

Coaches catalyze and encourage growth in leaders of groups and teams.

Did you catch the pivotal word in that definition? It's *growth*! The primary role of a coach in a leader's life is to foster that leader's growth. It's not administration. Not reporting. Not accountability. Not the latest church campaign or project. Those things may all be necessary components of the leader's growth. They may be on the punch list of activities that a coach needs to work through with a leader or team. But the primary purpose of a coach engaging in a leader's life is to catalyze and encourage growth.

Paul, one of the supreme models for coaching in the Bible, yearned to see his "children" grow in Christ. It was the driving passion in his life and often moved him deeply. "Oh, my dear children! I feel as if I'm going through labor pains for you again, and they will continue until Christ is fully developed in your lives" (Gal. 4:19 NLT).

A coach has the privilege of walking with a leader as he or she grows in many areas of life: as a leader, a Christ follower, a spouse, a parent, an employee. The list of growth areas is limited only by the depth of the trust relationship between the leader and the coach.

You Are a Growth Catalyst

As a coach, you will at times have the opportunity or need to catalyze growth in the life of a leader. God through the Holy Spirit causes all growth, but his primary means of causing that growth in us is through other people. People teach us, challenge us, help us, and correct us. They are catalytic to our growth.

Catalyze isn't an everyday word for most people, and it isn't understood completely by people who use it frequently! So what does it mean to be a catalyst as a coach? You can substitute other words for catalyze: cause, effect, initiate, or prompt. Those are all fitting words for a coach's impact, as sometimes a coach will need to prompt growth in a leader's life that isn't happening naturally, or at least initiate a conversation about that growth.

The word is most often used in the field of chemistry. *Dictionary.com* says a catalyst is "something used in small amounts that causes a reaction." When you introduce a catalyst into the equation, changes start to happen!

For people who do not come from the world of chemistry (like us), the hidden metaphors of a coach as a catalyst are rich in meaning. As you read the following descriptions of a chemical catalyst, think about the parallels to a coach's role in the life of a leader.

In a chemical reaction, the catalyst

- will participate in but is not consumed by the process;
- may participate in multiple transformations at one time;
- can speed up or slow down reactions around it;
- can provide alternative reaction pathways;
- can enable a reaction that would otherwise be blocked;
- can enable a reaction at lower temperatures.

The role of a chemical catalyst sounds a lot like that of effective, life-changing coaching! Sometimes a coach will recognize a growth edge for a leader long before the leader does. That growth edge may come in the form of a crisis or an opportunity. Situations will arise in the group that will require the leader to learn new skills and abilities. For whatever reason, the leader may be unable to see or seize the challenge to grow. In those moments, a wise coach is able to, *in small amounts*, offer wise counsel, guidance, and support that initiates a growth process for the leader.

You Encourage Leaders

Often what your leaders need most is not a catalytic word but an encouraging word. Leading a group can be a rewarding experience, but it can be draining as well. Sometimes your leaders are struggling just to stay in the game. At other times they will be thriving in areas of life and leadership. The truth is, what they need from you in the good times and the bad is encouragement. That's how God wired us.

It takes a coach to catalyze and encourage growth in the lives of leaders. The power of the Holy Spirit is released when someone speaks life and hope and truth into the heart of another person. This is especially true for leaders who carry the burden of ministry. They need words of life. Reflecting on the church leader's need for personal, soul-level support and authentic relationships, Larry Crabb writes, "Visionaries call us to religious action. Entrepreneurs figure out how to get the action going. Marketing geniuses brand the action till everybody's talking about it. Gifted performers speak or sing us into action. Again, all good things with an important place — but not first place. More important is that each leader be known by someone, not by a crowd or a committee, but by a person, a close friend, an intimate companion. And not merely held accountable, but genuinely known in an intimate, vulnerable, painfully real, long-term relationship" (*Soul Talk*, p. 53).

Not every coaching relationship will be as deep as Dr. Crabb longs for and describes. His point is well taken. Leaders need a person — a coach — to speak into their lives, to know them, love them, and support them. When this happens, the Holy Spirit seems to stir and awaken the leader. A leader feels cared for and understood, motivated to speak truth and life into the members of his or her group. Suddenly, ordinary people become extraordinary instruments in the hands of God.

When a dynamic leader emerges in a coaching relationship, it is exhilarating to watch, and to be a part of the process, as a coach. Most coaches can continue a long time on the encouragement from just one leader who understands and lives out Jesus's vision for community.

After interacting with hundreds of coaches through the years, we started to notice several qualities showing up repeatedly in coaches who developed these kinds of leaders. Because, if we are honest, not every coach-leader relationship produces an amazing partnership with a leader who will change the world — let alone his group. And not all of that is on the coach's shoulders. Some of that rests squarely on the leader and that person's effort, ability, spiritual maturity, and coachability, as well as the unseen factors that are there when two or three gather in Jesus's name. (You veterans of group life will understand what we mean.)

There are several qualities which greatly increase the likelihood that this partnership between a coach and leader can produce a positive, life-changing experience in groups and teams.

TEN QUALITIES OF HIGHLY EFFECTIVE COACHES

While not an exhaustive list, here are ten qualities we have found that highly effective coaches possess or can develop in their lives over time.

1. Life-changing coaches live with personal integrity. In his book *Leading from the Inside Out*, Samuel Rima writes, "The great apostle Paul lived with the constant awareness that his failure to manage his inner life well could actually result in his own personal stumbling, thus negatively affecting all he had worked so hard to accomplish as an apostle."

The same holds true for coaches. What you do and how you do it is an example to your leaders, so you need to pursue Christ and live with integrity. Living with integrity enables you to make statements like the ones made by Paul, who told the believers in Corith, "Follow my example, as I follow the example of Christ" (1 Cor. 11:1).

That's not to say that coaches should be perfect. No one is. The Latin root of the word *integrity* indicates a consistency in our lives—that we are acting according to the values, beliefs, and principles we claim to hold. A coach should think, speak, and behave in ways that are congruent to what he or she holds to be true and right. And that should be generally true of the coach's life at home, on the job, or wherever he or she is. Integrity is a lifestyle choice that coaches must make every day if they want to have lasting impact.

> The most important tool ultimately is the person and his or her makeup, yet it seems to get the least amount of attention and work.
>
> — Henry Cloud, Integrity

2. Life-changing coaches are passionate about developing leaders. The power of God working in one life has a ripple effect, producing results in each generation of leadership. When a coach has a passion to develop and support a leader, that leader will impact the lives of people in the small group he or she leads. And on it goes, like ripples traveling far beyond their point of origin in a tranquil lake.

Highly effective coaches recognize that their impact is multiplied through their strategic investment in people who are engaged in leadership or are emerging as new leaders. As you empower and encourage leaders, you are giving ministry into their hands, placing them on the front lines of effective shepherding. It's a ministry of reproduction.

3. Life-changing coaches are spiritually attuned. When the early church needed new leaders, its members carefully and prayerfully selected believers who had evidenced certain qualities—a faith firmly grounded in God's Word, a life showing solid character, and a heart filled with the Holy

Spirit and wisdom (Acts 6:1 – 7). As you follow the lives and ministries of these leaders, you see that their leadership was indeed Spirit-filled.

A coach's life and leadership needs to model these same qualities. The challenge of coaching small group leaders demands that you lean into the wisdom of God's Word and the power of the Holy Spirit. Coaches will not accomplish their ministry through their own might or power. Ministry can be done only through the strength and power given by God's Holy Spirit (Zech. 4:6).

Each of us is tempted at times to rely on our own skills, abilities, and experiences. While these will serve you well as a coach, they are not enough. This kind of Spiritless leadership will eventually leave us at the end of our resources. We will begin to mishandle challenges and overlook growth opportunities for the leaders in our care.

As Galatians 5:25 says, "Since we live by the Spirit, let us keep in step with the Spirit." Let's allow him to direct our conversation, our mentoring, and our relationship with each of our leaders. Staying attuned to the leading of God's Spirit is critical to life-changing coaching.

4. Life-changing coaches are self-starters. The role of a coach is among the volunteer roles that have the highest impact in the church. In many churches, discipleship, pastoral care, assimilation of new attendees, and other significant ministry activities are initiated or channeled through the group structure. The need for a coach to manage his or her personal life at a healthy pace, to stay connected to the leaders in his or her care, and to move forward on ministry priorities requires a person who can function with limited oversight and follow-up from church staff.

Coaches who thrive tend to be those who have more initiative, adaptability, and trustworthiness. They are able to stay focused in the middle of chaos or difficult challenges. These coaches follow through on tough stuff without a lot of outside encouragement. It's not because they *like* the tough stuff; it's because they find joy in the end result. They love to see leaders grow through the process of working through the tough challenges of leadership. These coaches jump into their task — that of developing people — with passion, energy, and initiative.

5. Life-changing coaches are intellectually curious. We were first introduced to the phrase "intellectual curiosity" some years ago through the research of the Hay McBer Group, a global human resources and management group based in Philadelphia. Their research has broad application regarding leadership in both the business and nonprofit sectors.

You can best capture the concept of being intellectually curious by thinking about your last meeting or social gathering where a good conversation took place. Who was the person in the room who kept asking the "Why?" question (if that person was also more than three years old)? Who was the person who kept asking deeper questions, not in an annoying way but in a good way? The person who kept peeling back the layers of the onion, searching for the heart of the issue, the central idea, the real wisdom in the conversation? That person probably has what could be described as intellectual curiosity: the desire to get to the right question as much as the right answer, to truly understand the situation and apply the right knowledge to achieve the best outcome.

You can see how this would be helpful for a coach. Coaches need to be ever learning, ever curious about the leadership role and about how to improve as a catalyst and encourager of growth. They need to look at problems and opportunities as they arise with a leader, and not simply jump on the first answer as the best answer. They are wired so that they must continue to ask questions, to seek to fully understand each situation and all its complexity. They will think and pray through situations afterward, reflecting on how God might have used them differently or how he might continue to use the situation to shape the leader or the group.

6. Life-changing coaches are others-focused. Name the top ten places you would look in the Bible for passages on being others-focused, and it's doubtful that the book of Ezekiel would make the list. Yet in Ezekiel 34, God clearly spells out his heart for how he wants a shepherding leader to think and behave.

Through Ezekiel, God indicts the leaders of Israel. He names the things the leaders have done wrong in caring for and leading the nation. Near the top of the list is that instead of being others-focused, the leaders have been self-centered (Ezek. 34:8), caring only for themselves and ignoring the needs of the people. God goes on to condemn and punish these leaders for their lack of compassion and leadership.

To be effective as coaches, we need to be focused on the needs of our small group leaders. It's the same "I come to serve, not to be served" approach that Jesus had to his ministry (Mark 10:45).

What does it look like to be an others-focused coach? In Ezekiel, after condemning the leaders of Israel, God delivers an amazing speech. He defines what it means to be an others-focused leader, spelling out the actions he is going to take as the new leader and shepherd of the nation (Ezek. 34:11 – 16 MSG).

In this passage, God says he will

- "rescue them from all the places they've been scattered to in the storms";

- "feed them on the mountains of Israel";
- "lead them into lush pasture";
- "make sure they get plenty of rest";
- "go after the lost";
- "collect the strays";
- "doctor the injured";
- "build up the weak ones";
- "oversee the strong ones so they're not exploited."

That's a remarkable list. God gives us a model for what it means to be an others-focused coach. Good coaches know well the challenges of leadership and stay in close contact with their leaders. Over time, they come to know when their leaders need praise and when they need to be challenged, when they are injured or weak and when they are strong.

An others-focused coach will fight the urge to make coaching conversations about himself or herself. Instead the coach will listen more than he or she talks, working to discern what God may be up to in the leader's life.

This kind of coach will hang in there with a leader when a crisis comes in their life or their group, walking with them through their dark valley. The dark valleys of leadership do come. Leaders and group members will have struggles. People sin. Relationships break. Life happens. Coaches who have this others-focused mentality will keep their fingers on the pulse of their leaders' life and ministry. They will have a sense of each leader's unique spiritual and developmental needs so they can invest the right energy, time, and resources to help each leader grow.

7. Life-changing coaches are relationally savvy. Matthew records these words about the ministry of Jesus: "A bruised reed he will not break, and a smoldering wick he will not snuff out" (Matt. 12:20). It's easy to overlook the relational awareness embedded in those words.

We can understand the compassion, the tenderness, of Jesus. We can easily see it in the miracles he performed, hear it in his teachings, and see it modeled in his daily life.

We understand how he could forgive Peter for denying him three times in the courtyard that night while Jesus was being tried in front of the Sanhedrin. But it's easy to miss the *way* that Jesus emphasized that forgiveness to Peter. The threefold affirmation of Peter's love for Jesus in John 21 was Jesus's way of strengthening a bruised reed, a smoldering wick.

Jesus knew that this young leader had to be struggling after his failure in the courtyard. Peter needed affirmation that he was forgiven, that he could still be used by God, that he had not forfeited his calling with one night of weakness. Had Jesus not been relationally aware, Peter may never have recovered from this devastating failure. This bruised reed may have broken completely.

In the foreword to Steve Saccone's book *Relational Intelligence*, Erwin McManus writes, "Many leaders see the goals clearly, but are visually impaired when it comes to people" (p. xiii). That ought never to be true of coaches! Coaches must work to develop a relational awareness, so they know when to challenge and when to encourage their leaders.

8. Life-changing coaches are effective communicators. Seldom if ever will a coach be involved in communicating to large audiences. Most of your communication will be in smaller settings or one-on-one. That type of communication involves a specific set of skills, many of which a coach may have already developed as a small group leader.

Top on that list of skills is being an active listener. James 1:19 emphasizes the need: "Everyone should be quick to listen, slow to speak and slow to become angry." Active listening involves focusing your attention on the person speaking rather than on how you will respond. It also involves watching body language, listening to tone of voice, asking good questions —all those skills you have been using for years as a group leader. Listening to your leaders with empathy and understanding will show them that you care about them as more than just a name on your organizational chart.

Life-changing coaches are able to communicate clearly and effectively with their leaders. That involves giving constructive feedback on how they are progressing as leaders, communicating the vision and values of the church and the small group ministry, and talking leaders through the tough situations and messes that come up in every small group.

9. Life-changing coaches are truth tellers. Once you have built trust with your leaders, once they are known and loved, you can begin to speak gracious, transforming words of truth into their lives. This can be one of the most challenging skills for many coaches to develop. Please understand: truth telling is not about conflict resolution.

The roots of truth telling are found in 2 Timothy 4:2, where Paul writes, "Correct, rebuke and encourage—with great patience and careful instruction."

Sometimes truth telling involves a corrective word, sometimes a warning, sometimes teaching, and sometimes strong encouragement. It can be used to point out destructive behaviors or attitudes. It can serve to challenge someone to the next step of growth.

And the truth should always be spoken in love (Eph. 4:15). Emily Dickinson once said, "Tell the truth, but tell it slant." She was not advising us to be less than honest. Rather she was indicating that we can convey what we mean without being hurtful.

The truth can be communicated in a loving way. Truth not rooted in love will feel like criticism or faultfinding. It has a harsh, brutal edge and has the potential to destroy the coaching relationship.

10. Life-changing coaches are inspiring. Often, people serving in the church hunger for meaning or purpose. They can feel disconnected from the overall vision of the church, lost and confused, performing what may seem to be random or tedious tasks that have no connection to the church's overall vision.

No one likes tedious, meaningless tasks. We will sometimes put up with them for a paycheck, but we won't tolerate them for long when we are volunteering. We will find somewhere else to invest our discretionary time.

What happens when the task is connected to the vision? Leaders will make significant sacrifices, knowing they are doing something worthy of their best selves because they are doing something vital, even holy.

Coaches inspire leaders. They make a direct connection between the everyday tasks of leading a small group and the broader vision for community. Coaches help leaders catch and carry out the vision of the real-life change that is possible when people encounter God's presence in the company of friends. Coaches envision what is possible and infuse energy into that vision. They inspire longtime leaders to stay in the game, and emerging leaders to become active players.

TIME FOR A CHECKUP: TWO TOOLS

It's time to reflect on how you are doing in developing these ten qualities in your life as a coach. As you do, remember that it's normal for coaches to be strong in some areas and weaker in others. The important thing here is to be aware of your weaknesses and begin to grow and to develop those qualities.

Included are two tools you can use for this checkup. The first is a self-evaluation tool (p. 38). The best time to use this tool is when you have a block of time to pray and reflect on the past few months of your life and ministry as a coach.

The second tool is a leader feedback tool (p. 39). It offers you the opportunity to have the leaders in your care give you their feedback on your efforts as a coach. This tool would best be used after you have established a relationship with them over several months.

Copy this page and have each leader fill it out and return it either to you or, if you prefer, to a staff member who can compile the feedback and give you an overview of the results. The combined feedback from both tools can be very helpful in showing you areas where you have strengths as a coach as well as areas where you need to grow or improve.

SELF-EVALUATION TOOL

Carefully evaluate each of the ten coaching qualities below. Spend some time thinking and praying about the last six months. If it would be helpful, you may want to write some notes in a journal (or on p. 40).

In the box to the left of each quality, draw one of the following symbols to represent the growth trend in your life or in your coaching over the past six months.

- ⬆ If you feel your growth has been positive
- ⬇ If you feel your growth has been negative
- ➡ If you feel you have not changed

	Personal integrity *Am I living according to the values, beliefs, and principles I claim to hold?*
	Passionate about developing leaders *Am I consistently investing in existing and emerging leaders?*
	Spiritually attuned *Am I leaning into the wisdom of God's Word and the power of the Holy Spirit as I coach?*
	Self-starter *Am I coaching with initiative, adaptability, and trustworthiness?*
	Intellectually curious *Am I consistently searching for the heart of the issue in order to achieve the best outcome?*
	Others-focused *Am I working to discern what God may be up to in each leader's life?*
	Relationally savvy *Am I aware of when to challenge and when to encourage my leaders?*
	Effective communicator *Am I listening well and communicating clearly with my leaders?*
	Truth teller *Am I conveying what needs to be said without being hurtful?*
	Inspiring *Am I helping leaders make a direct connection between the leadership tasks and the broader vision for community?*

LEADER FEEDBACK TOOL

Thanks for your willingness to complete this feedback tool for your coach. It is an important part of his or her growth and development.

Carefully evaluate each of the ten coaching qualities below. Spend some time thinking and praying about your interaction with your coach over the past few months.

In the box to the left of each quality, draw one of the following symbols to represent your understanding of the growth trend in the coach's life or in his or her coaching relationship with you during recent months.

⬆ If you feel your coach's growth has been positive

⬇ If you feel your coach's growth has been negative

➡ If you feel your coach has not changed

	Personal integrity *Is your coach living according to the values, beliefs, and principles he or she claims to hold?*
	Passionate about developing leaders *Is your coach consistently investing in you as a leader?*
	Spiritually attuned *Is your coach leaning into the wisdom of God's Word and the power of the Holy Spirit as he or she coaches?*
	Self-starter *Is your coach coaching with initiative, adaptability, and trustworthiness?*
	Intellectually curious *Is your coach consistently searching for the heart of the issue in order to achieve the best outcome?*
	Others-focused *Is your coach working to discern what God may be up to in your life as a leader?*
	Relationally savvy *Is your coach aware of when to challenge and when to encourage you as a leader?*
	Effective communicator *Is your coach listening well and communicating clearly with you as a leader?*
	Truth teller *Is your coach conveying what needs to be said without being hurtful?*
	Inspiring *Is your coach helping you make a direct connection between the leadership tasks and the broader vision for community?*

Additional comments or thoughts:

Chapter 2

COACHING'S CORE PRACTICES

If you want to master anything, you must begin by mastering "the core." Focus first on what lies at the heart of the ministry, the sport, the business, the hobby. Don't get distracted with secondary issues before gaining proficiency with the core.

If we were teaching you to play baseball, we would teach you how to throw, catch, hit, and run the bases. Major deficiencies in any of those four key areas will prevent you from becoming a solid performer in baseball (unless you're a major-league pitcher).

At the bank where Bill worked shortly after college, there were three core practices. Neglecting any one of the three or poor performance in any area would result in big trouble. The three areas: collect deposits, manage cash, and make quality loans.

Let's face it: if no one deposits money in your bank, you have a problem. If you fail to effectively manage the money people deposit, you have another problem. If you make frivolous loans to people or businesses that can't pay you back, you have ... well, you'll soon discover you don't have a bank anymore!

The same is true in music. If you play an instrument such as the guitar or piano, you must be able to read notes, manage the tempo, and master the fingering patterns. So you practice scales every day. The core matters!

The core of coaching focuses on three practices:

1. *Discover.* This practice requires active listening and asking many questions. Your focus here is to be a learner before being a teacher. The leader—not your agenda—is job one.
2. *Develop.* Everyone needs and longs for personal development, but few people have someone who will take time to invest in them. Once you have an idea of what a leader needs and how to serve that person, you

can help develop a plan for his or her personal growth and ministry success.

3. *Dream.* It's easy to get so bogged down in the logistics and demands of coaching that you and your leaders alike can lose the big picture. Dreaming together allows you to keep your head up and your eyes focused on the kingdom work God is doing.

We call it 3-D coaching. If you look carefully, you'll see that the 3-D framework was used when coaching Chad. Oh, it was never mentioned specifically ("Now, Chad, let's move into part 2 of the 3-D coaching strategy and talk about ..."). Thank goodness! But it was embedded in the approach.

REFLECTION

Briefly skim through Chad and Eric's story again. Provide examples of where parts of the 3-D strategy were being used.

Discover:

Develop:

Dream:

CORE PRACTICE 1. DISCOVER

Who is this leader, how is the person's spiritual life, and what kind of ministry does he or she have?

To discover what a leader needs requires genuine care and listening. Back in chapter 1, it was clear that Chad's coaches sought to understand Chad, his group, and his relationship with God. Whether it was conversations at the café or quick emails, coaches made a point to know him as a person—not simply as a leader on an organizational chart.

First, Create a Culture of Trust

Building trust with leaders that will help you *discover* what is going on with them and with their groups? Here are four simple, focused activities that will create the right environment for discovery and dialogue.

1. Build real relationships
2. Listen deeply
3. Be an encourager
4. Provide care

Build Real Relationships

In his ministry, Jesus placed a high priority on relationships. He built strong relationships during the time he spent with the Twelve. That was Jesus's plan from the beginning. Consider the relational component in these passages:

Mark 3:14: Jesus calls the Twelve for two purposes: to be with him and to do ministry. The first priority is relationships—the "be with" factor. J. B. Phillips' translation says Jesus calls them to be his regular "companions."

John 14:3: To calm their fears, Jesus assures the Twelve that he will return for them one day. Why? So they can be with him.

John 15:15: At the Last Supper, Jesus says, "I no longer call you servants … Instead, I have called you friends."

John 17:24: Just hours before his death, Jesus prays in the garden. One of his deepest longings is for the Twelve to be with him again in heaven.

Forming an authentic relationship is the first step to intentionally shepherding your leaders. Leaders want to be built into, cared for, and loved. Leaders want to establish trust, open communication, and form genuine relationships. They first want to have a shepherd who feeds them rather than a supervisor who leads them.

Coaching requires an understanding of the feed-lead ratio. Leaders consistently express a desire to be fed by their coaches. They want a coach who seeks to understand them—their walk with God, their family life, and their relationship to the church. They long for someone who helps them discern next steps of personal spiritual growth.

Initially, at least, leaders are looking for this feeding aspect to comprise about 80 percent of the coach-leader relationship. The other 20 percent is leadership, providing the vision and the skills necessary to carry out the role of group leader. Over time, you will see this ratio begin to shift. As trust builds, the leadership component can increase, but never to the point that it outweighs the shepherding component.

> Remember: Honor the 80:20 feed-lead ratio!

It will take time and intentionality to develop a relationship with each of your leaders. A coach needs to consistently seek to understand the whole picture of who each one is, both as a person and as a leader. As you build trust with the leader, ask deeper questions that uncover their thoughts, beliefs, and feelings. Ask questions that will help you:

Understand their spiritual journey. (How did they come to Christ? To your church? Who has been influential in their journey?)

Understand their life history. (What was and is their family like? How did they celebrate? How did they grieve? How did they handle conflict? What were the major turning points in their life?)

Understand their heart. (What brings them joy? What makes them sad? What do they dream about?)

While the primary tool to build relationships will be one-on-one time, you can also plan activities to foster relationships with your leaders during huddle times. (For ideas on how to utilize each of these settings, see chapter 3, "The Coach's Toolbox.")

Listen Deeply

Whether the conversation is a planned one-on-one time or a chance meeting, coaches need to practice good listening skills. As you shepherd your leaders, here are some guidelines.

- *Listen more than you speak.* Don't interrupt or look for openings in the conversation to get your point across. "Everyone should be quick to listen, slow to speak and slow to become angry" (James 1:19).
- *Actively engage in their story.* As leaders share their story, do not become preoccupied with pondering your next question or response.

- *Ask for clarification.* When what they are communicating is not clear to you, don't presume to know what they are trying to say.
- *Keep the focus on them.* Resist the urge to use their story as a springboard to tell your experiences. Use your stories and experiences sparingly and only when doing so will be helpful to the leader's growth.
- *Fight the temptation to move too quickly to solutions.* Seek to listen and fully understand. "Answering before listening is both stupid and rude" (Prov. 18:13 MSG).
- *Listen beyond their words.* Pay attention to their body language, facial expressions, tone of voice, and choice of words. These nonverbal cues can help you discern unexpressed thoughts, feelings, and struggles.
- *Ask permission to move deeper.* Ask questions that get beyond surface conversation and offer the opportunity to share feelings, opinions, and values. Try to move from self-description to self-disclosure.
- *When your mind wanders, confess it.* Everyone has those moments when their mind drifts. Generally, people can tell if you aren't really listening. When it happens to you, honestly tell the leader, ask them to forgive you, and encourage them to repeat what they shared.

Be an Encourager

Leading a group can be a rewarding experience. Leaders help people form new friendships, and they watch those relationships grow. They see people come to Christ and grow in their devotion to him. They develop and launch new leaders.

Group leadership can also be very challenging. Seemingly fantastic plans for a group meeting may flop. Members will miss meetings. People work late, they take vacations, or their kids get sick. At times, relational harmony will give way to chaos. Conflict will happen. Group members will move away or quit. Groups birth. Groups end. Some group members grow spiritually, while some seem to grow stagnant.

In the tough times, a word of encouragement can mean the difference between a leader staying in the game and a leader quitting. The truth is, we all need encouragement.

Throughout Scripture, good leaders have modeled encouragement for us.

- At God's command, Moses encouraged his apprentice, Joshua (Deut. 1:38; 3:28).
- King Hezekiah encouraged people who were giving their lives in service to the Lord (2 Chron. 30:22).
- Josiah encouraged the spiritual leaders of Israel (2 Chron. 35:2).

- A major portion of Paul's writing and ministry to churches was encouragement (Acts 14:22; 16:40; 20:1–2; 27:36).
- One leader, Joseph, did this so well that the apostles gave him a new name: Barnabas (Acts 4:36). Literally translated, it means "son of encouragement." Later we find him living up to the new name as he encouraged the churches (Acts 11:23).

Leaders need their coach to be a Barnabas for them. They need encouragement to continue to grow spiritually, and they need you to offer words of encouragement on a regular basis. Leaders have expressed that what they desire most from their coach is spiritual development skills. Gain their permission and their trust to serve as a guide—not an expert—for the next leg of their spiritual journey, and check in with them regularly regarding their personal spiritual growth.

- In what spiritual disciplines and practices are your leaders regularly engaging?
- Have they drifted away from God? At times, we all stray and need a guiding hand and loving encouragement to return to God.
- Where do they sense God is leading them to grow next? Help them discern what their growth edges could be.
- What could a next step of spiritual growth look like? Rather than tell them what to do, brainstorm a list of possibilities. Explore together what new spiritual disciplines or practices could help their growth.

Beyond guidance in spiritual growth, group leaders need encouragement in their leadership skills. They need a coach who will do the following:

- Offer encouragement for things they have done well, even little things.
- Praise them when they tackle difficult issues and challenges. Even though they may not complete every detail perfectly, find the things leaders do well and offer genuine praise.
- Encourage them to persevere in the tough times and not get tired of doing the right things. They'll see the benefits in time if they don't get discouraged and give up (Gal. 6:9).
- Use a variety of encouragement styles. Personally written letters, cards, and even email notes are a great source of encouragement to leaders. Recognition in front of their peers can also be important.
- Discover their unique leadership gifts and potential.
- When appropriate, offer public praise or even awards. A great time for this is in your leadership gatherings. Sharing the struggles and

successes your leaders experience can deepen community and cast vision for the kind of groups and leaders you hope to develop.

Most change happens slowly, over time. So as you encourage growth in your leaders, remember Paul's words: "Be prepared in season and out of season; correct, rebuke and encourage—with great patience and careful instruction" (2 Tim. 4:2).

Provide Care

Your leaders will eventually encounter pain, loss, and disappointment in their own lives or in the life of a group member. In those seasons, leaders may need guidance from you. They may need help determining how best to care for group members who are in crisis. This is especially true for

- leaders who have never walked through a crisis with a group;
- newly formed groups, where the relationships are still developing;
- extreme crises, such as the death of a group member or a catastrophic loss.

If the crisis is in the leader's personal life or family, the leader needs you to be a pastor to him or her—a caring shepherd. It may be helpful for you to offer guidance to the group members, encouraging them to care for their leader. Whether it's a leader or a group member who's in need, remember:

- Hurting people value your presence over your words or skills. A call or visit can be very encouraging.
- Pray for and with people, asking God to restore their physical and spiritual health.
- Look for any ways you might serve them. Do they need help with household chores, family responsibilities, or food? Do they need help with transportation?
- Remember that shared pain is often the gateway to growth. This is often true not only for the individual but also for the group.
- Know when to ask for help. Sometimes a particular need will be so large that the group won't be able to meet it. Know where you or your leaders can turn for assistance in your church.

The natural tendency for most people is to withdraw from, not move toward, people who are in pain. By your example, encourage leaders to come alongside people who are hurting. Guide leaders as they develop their heart of compassion.

REFLECTION

Among the four areas listed below, what are your strengths and where do you need development? (Sometime after completing this reflection, ask people who lead you and people you coach what they perceive as your strong areas and your areas for development).

1. Build relationships

My thoughts:

What others say:

2. Listen deeply

My thoughts:

What others say:

3. Be an encourager

My thoughts:

What others say:

4. Provide care

My thoughts:

What others say:

Next, Focus on the Key Areas of a Leader's Life

As you build a culture of trust and safety, begin to *discover* the areas in which a leader needs support, growth, and encouragement, so you can *dream* with them about God's work through them and *develop* them in their leadership.

Your mission is to enter the world of a group leader and discover their story as it relates to

1. their *personal life* as a leader;
2. their *spiritual life* with God and what he is doing in them;
3. their *ministry life* as they work with members of their group.

1. Personal Life

Coaches care about a leader's heart, mind, and soul. This is not an investigation and not an interrogation; it's a *conversation*. In chapter 3, we will help you with some specific kinds of conversations you must navigate with leaders. For now, let's focus on the kinds of questions to ask a leader as you build a relationship with them. The more you get to know them, the more they will trust you.

The personal life of a leader lies at the heart of their ministry and life. By showing interest about this area, you are saying, "I want to know your world and your story—at any level you want to discuss it—because you are a unique creation of God and deeply valued and loved."

Granted, this may be awkward for you. This is not a probe. It's an invitation to a leader to open up their heart to you, to view you as a friend and confidant, a prayer partner and advocate.

Here are some general guidelines for discussing personal life issues.

1. *Seek first to understand rather than to be understood.* We tend to be eager to share wisdom, solve problems, and suggest advice before we fully understand the leader and what's going on inside them. Don't assume—ask.

2. *Ask permission before asking a personal question.* "May I ask you about your work environment? It sounds like a challenging place." "May I spend a few moments unpacking what you just told me about growing up on the East Coast? It must have been hard to lose your father at a young age in a tough city." By asking permission, we allow the leader an out or at least show that we want to honor their desire to keep parts of their story to themselves.

3. *Invite conversation; don't force it.* "I'd like to know more about that." "I wonder how that must have felt?" These kinds of statements show you are listening but aren't as direct as "Explain that to me" or "What exactly was that conversation about?"

4. *Use open or hypothetical questions that allow for a range of responses.* "How do you think your experience as the only woman in a management role at your company will help you relate to other women in the marketplace?" By giving lots of room for an answer, you allow the leader to gauge their own level of comfort and safety in the conversation.

5. *Always acknowledge and affirm the risk a leader has taken in opening their life.* Make sure the leader knows that *you* know how scary it was to share a part of himself or herself with you. Especially in a new coaching relationship. Trust takes time and requires constant nurturing. "Thanks for telling me about that struggle with your girlfriend. Rest assured, I will keep that in confidence and also in my prayers for you. I am honored you would tell me about that."

2. Spiritual Life

We know that all of life is spiritual, but use the term *spiritual* to focus on a leader's relationship with God. This relationship is where leaders will draw strength, find hope, and experience growth or frustration. It is also a delicate area for some to discuss, so the five guidelines would apply here.

Here are some key areas in which to engage in conversation with a leader.

Image of God. How does the leader see God and relate to him (as Judge, Friend, Lover, Leader, Helper)?

Prayer life. Is the leader stuck, engaged, feeling connected?

Bible reading. How does the leader use devotional reading, Bible study, meditation on Scripture, Bible memory, and so on?

Worship. Does the leader participate in regular gatherings for worship? Does he or she view all of life as worship and devotion to God?

Spiritual practices. What other practices does the leader know or use (fasting, silence, solitude, service, giving, and so on)?

3. Ministry Life

Now that you have been getting to know the leader's personal story and spiritual needs, let's turn toward some conversations about the group he or she leads. How is the ministry really going? What resources, help, or support can you bring to the leader?

Leaders often have a variety of needs but seldom express those freely to a coach. Usually this is because the relationship is not deep enough yet, and perhaps there is a fear of judgment if things are not going well. If you recall again the conversation between Chad and Eric, there was an awkward interaction at the beginning of the relationship. That's normal. A leader will usually have some fears or concerns about sharing his or her ministry with a coach. Here are some common ones.

1. *"My coach doesn't know my group members, so how can he/she understand my leadership needs?"* This is true, and that's why coaches are encouraged to visit groups or to meet the members in other settings at church or in the community. The more a coach understands the context of the leader's work, the better help he or she can give. Coaching is a relational ministry. The more you know the leader and the group, the more leadership insights you can provide. But what is also true is that coaches work with multiple groups. Problems, principles, and lessons learned from interaction with other leaders will become a rich pool of resources from which you can draw to help each group in your care.

2. *"I don't need another boss; I already have one at work."* The leader is right. And that's the last thing most coaches want to be—a boss or

a spy or a judge. You must work hard to communicate that you are a friend, a partner, an encourager, a resource person, a fellow leader. You are not in a leader's life to critique and evaluate. You are there to build them up and connect them with people and resources for their success. It's important to clarify your role and relationship with the leader. You will have to explain why you are there and why you are doing this ministry. And tell them what you are *not* there to do, just to be clear.

3. *"I have some tough issues in my group; will my coach understand how to handle those issues?"* Maybe a coach will have a great insight into a leader's worst problems, and maybe he or she won't. But a good coach will find someone who can help — another coach, another group leader, a pastor, or other wise counsel. A coach is not a know-it-all but should be competent to seek out answers and rally support to a leader, regardless of the need or crisis the group is facing.

4. *"I'm doing just fine, and so is my group. Why do I need a coach right now?"* This is probably the most common remark from group leaders. Since there are no immediate crises in the group and people seem generally happy, there appears to be no need for coaching. But as we mentioned early in chapter 1, even people who are at the top of their game — athletes, CEOs, musicians, educators, actors — use coaches on a regular basis for feedback, for insight, for problem solving, and for finding the best resources to help them pursue success. We have to gently remind leaders that "fine" may not be enough. God wants our best, and a group deserves a leader who is growing personally and spiritually, not one who is just cruising along, leading average meetings and offering spiritual leftovers to members.

Encourage a leader to discuss the group's progress to see where there are opportunities for deeper devotion to God, for creative outreach, for retreats, for service to others, and for new ways to engage the Bible. There are some very helpful and creative ideas and resources in *Leading Life-Changing Small Groups*. Encourage a leader to use such a manual for his or her personal and ministry growth.

CORE PRACTICE 2. DEVELOP

As you equip leaders with key skills, you are helping them become more effective in meeting the real needs of their small group members. Remember how Priscilla and Aquila were influential in equipping Apollos (Acts 18:23–28). Though Apollos was already eloquent, instructed in the Word, fervent in spirit, and able to teach, he needed more training from this couple to improve and develop. All leaders need to improve their skills, even leaders who are well equipped and seasoned in the Lord.

So as you shepherd and guide your leaders, try to discern their growth edges. What are their strengths and weaknesses? Make some personal notes along the way. These insights will prove valuable later. As the trust between you builds, leaders will begin to share struggles or challenges they are facing in their groups. In that moment, they are signaling that they are open to helpful ideas that will better equip them for leadership.

Why Focus on Skills?

If coaching is mostly about relationships, why focus on skills?

While the relationship with your leaders is important, don't get stuck there. It's easy to make the mistake of turning the coach-leader relationship into nothing more than a deep friendship. A coach can spend years with a leader only to realize that they have cared for their needs without developing their skills. They have forged a good friendship but have done little to improve the leader's ability. The balance between shepherding and equipping is hard to maintain.

Building a caring, nurturing relationship with your leaders is important. In fact, this shepherding relationship is foundational to all your work with them. When that relationship is growing, leaders can begin to identify skills they will need to learn or improve upon in order to take steps toward achieving the vision. When a leader recognizes a leadership gap, it can serve as a strong internal motivator and create a hunger for learning.

Developing leaders is an exciting and rewarding aspect of coaching. The better you understand a leader and their group context, the clearer you will be about their growth opportunities. It is not essential that you alone are "the developer" responsible for crafting and executing an in-depth training plan for every leader you work with. But you can do a lot to further a leader's development and growth. That was the focus of Eric, Sean, and Allison, the coaches who built into the life of Chad.

GUIDELINES FOR EQUIPPING YOUR LEADERS

Affirm their gifts and abilities. Every leader will have strengths and weaknesses. Make sure to affirm your leaders and encourage ongoing development of their talents. Offer a balance of building into their strengths and shoring up their weaknesses. Consider asking leaders to share from their strengths in a leadership gathering, as a way to develop others.

Teach from their experiences. Every experience — good and bad — provides an opportunity to learn. Listen for common themes to emerge from the groups you coach. As leaders share with you, watch for specific examples that can serve as a learning experience for all your leaders.

Discern their growth edges. Over time, you will begin to observe areas that are consistently challenging for a group leader. You may see unhealthy patterns developing in their personal walk or in their leadership of the group. Offer resources and tools to develop their skills and abilities in these areas.

Solve problems with them. Problem solving requires listening and understanding. Work to identify possible solutions, and help leaders decide which would be best for their small group. You may need to consult with a staff member or small group point person before committing to a plan.

Utilize role plays. Role plays are especially effective in helping leaders learn interpersonal skills. They can be highly effective in teaching leaders skills like conflict resolution, active listening, and asking effective questions.

Learn together. You can't know the answer to every issue or problem your leaders will encounter. So when you don't know, admit it! Work together with a leader to find the answer through the Bible, another leader, a fellow coach, a staff member, or some other resource.

Connect Leaders to Training Opportunities

There are four major ways in which leaders grow and develop in their ministry skills.

Classroom	On-the-job
Self-directed	Coach-mentor

Classroom

Leaders need clarity and motivation. Many churches offer training classes, especially for new leaders. Sometimes this is an orientation, sometimes a Saturday morning, sometimes several hours of classes held throughout the week or during an adult Sunday school hour. Make sure you are aware of what is being offered and how it might serve your leaders. Then, as you get to know your leaders and their needs for growth, you can recommend current or upcoming classes. These might address needs in any of the areas you focused on when you were in discover mode—personal life, spiritual life, and ministry life.

Skill training and motivational classes in these areas provide your leaders opportunities for growth, for meeting other small group leaders, for connecting with church-wide ministry staff or leaders, and for stretching their minds and hearts.

Typically, the classes with names like "How to Lead a Small Group" or "How to Coach Leaders" are designed for newer leaders and coaches. You and your leaders can take advantage of these.

Self-Directed

Leaders are learners. They understand that reading, studying, or listening to good teaching is part of the growth process. Throughout this manual are many resources that you can recommend to leaders.

Self-directed learning—using books, listening to teaching on a CD or online, watching a teaching video, talking to other experienced coaches and leaders—is the responsibility of every leader. Encourage your leaders to be working through some material on their own.

We have discovered that giving leaders too many options overwhelms them. So make clear recommendations for areas of need or growth. Saying, "There are lots of books about prayer at the Christian bookstore and online!" is not the way to help a leader. Be specific; tell them how the resources you advocate will help, and offer to walk through the resource with a leader so they understand how to use it.

Newer leaders tend to spend most of their training time on the left side of the chart on page 54—in the classroom and with self-directed activities. As leaders develop, however, they will likely learn more by leading a group (on-the-job) and by gaining feedback from others (coach-mentor).

On-the-Job

Leaders learn by leading. On-the-job leadership sharpens your mind and shapes your character. It requires you to put your theology in action and provides an environment for immediate feedback. A quick look around the room lets you know how well that last icebreaker idea really worked or how effective that new approach to group prayer really turned out to be.

This is true for your leaders, and it is true for you. You become a great coach by coaching—or at least you have a better shot at it. We are assuming that someone is giving you feedback and a place to process what you are learning on the job.

Coach-Mentor

Leaders need support. Some of the best long-term training a leader receives is from a coach or mentor—someone like you. On-the-job training gives a leader experience. But experience that is not evaluated is dangerous. Leaders may develop bad habits and ministry styles they keep repeating, thinking they are doing well.

How many of us have had teachers or professors who had an awkward or ineffective teaching style that had never been critiqued? A professor in my master's program would read his outline to the class—line by line. "Point A.1.—God is powerful. Point A.1.a.—God's power is unlimited." Ad infinitum, ad nauseum.

Students waited all semester to fill out his teacher evaluation, only to discover he had tenure and was no longer subject to evaluation by students. Great system—it perpetuates ineffectiveness. The class was mostly a waste of time. He could have handed out copies of the outline, and students could have had many fruitful discussions. But no one, apparently, gave him the feedback he needed or held him accountable to change his style.

Coaches like you are invaluable to leaders. You provide the conversations, feedback, new ideas, and fresh vision leaders need for growth.

REFLECTION

Each leader is unique and needs different training experiences. Think of your leaders and place their names next to the training environments that might be best for them.

Classroom:

Self-directed:

On-the-job:

Coach-mentor:

CORE PRACTICE 3. DREAM

"Some of us let great dreams die, but others nourish and protect them; nurse them through bad days till they bring them to the sunshine and light which comes always to those who sincerely hope that their dreams will come true" (Woodrow Wilson).

To dream is a gift from God, the product of the imagination and creativity he gave us when making us in his image. Life pressures, ministry demands, and personal challenges afford us little time or energy for dreaming. We ask, "How can I even think about the future when the present is so full of activity and I am still cleaning up messes from my past?"

Wilson was right. We have to nurse the dreams we have, because they become sickly and die young. Dreaming allows your leaders to set their sights high, on God's kingdom vision for his church and for their ministry. Asking, "What if ..." or saying, "Imagine what the group might be like if ..." is as critical to a leader as having competence and skill for his or her work.

> Without dreams, work and ministry can become drudgery!

So allow yourself to dream for a moment. When you think of a life-changing small group, what images come to mind?

- How do the members interact with each other?
- How do they care for one another? Serve one another? Encourage one another?
- In what ways are they meeting needs in the church and in the community at large?
- What would your church be like if every group functioned this way?

That's the basic concept behind vision. Any vision for community begins with a picture of what small groups would be like and how leaders would function in an ideal world.

Having a clear vision will affect your interaction with your leaders. It will impact your conversations with them, the resources you provide for them—even how you pray for them.

So when it comes to small groups, what's your vision? Again, take a moment and dream. What is your current vision for group life and how community, when practiced in a group, can change lives? Write some of your thoughts below. Then, after you think through your personal vision, we will guide you through the process of helping your leaders have a vision.

REFLECTION

My vision for group life:

Helping Your Leaders Find a Vision

Most churches have a vision for the role small groups will play in their church. The vision often breaks down when it gets translated from a larger vision (what community looks like in the church as a whole) to the role each group and leader can play in helping the church realize that vision.

Coaches can easily fall into the trap of simply serving as a conduit for vision, parroting to small group leaders the vision of the church. If that happens, the vision will not capture the leaders' hearts, and there will be little connection between the vision and the leaders' day-to-day activities. Instead of merely casting vision to your leaders, create space for them to think about or dream about their group. Work with your leaders to create a clear and compelling vision for each of their groups—one that captures their hearts and motivates them to action.

The Power of Vision

A vision has tremendous power when it's clear and compelling. It creates a hunger in us for something richer, fuller, or deeper than what we are currently experiencing. It draws out our best thinking and energy.

Vision has the ability to do the following:

Give meaning. It helps leaders understand that group life is about more than leading a meeting; it's about life change.

Create hunger. It helps leaders grasp the bigger ideas of the mission of the church and the call to community. The gap between their skills and what's required to achieve the vision will create a hunger for training and coaching.

Change focus. Vision can turn leaders' focus from themselves and their group members to the needs of people outside Christ and his community.

Give hope. Leaders need hope; they need to know they can do this. God painted for Abraham a vision of a mighty nation coming through his bloodline. "Against all hope, Abraham in hope believed" (Rom. 4:18). Vision inspired hope; hope enabled Abraham to believe and achieve the vision.

In the book *Organizing Genius*, Warren Bennis illustrates the power of vision with an account from one of the scientists who served on the Manhattan Project, building the world's first nuclear bomb. The best and brightest engineers in the country were recruited for the project.

> They were assigned to work on the primitive computers of the period, doing energy calculations and other tedious jobs. But the army, obsessed with security, refused to tell them anything specific about the project. They didn't know that they were building a weapon that could end the war or even what their calculations meant. They were simply expected to do the work, which they did—slowly and not very well. Feynman, who supervised the technicians, prevailed on his superiors to tell the recruits what they were doing and why.
>
> Permission was granted to lift the veil of secrecy, and Oppenheimer gave them a special lecture on the nature of the project and their own contribution.
>
> "Complete transformation," Feynman recalled. "They began to invent ways of doing it better. They improved the scheme. They worked at night. They didn't need supervising in the night; they didn't need anything.
>
> "They understood everything; they invented several of the programs that we used." Ever the scientist, Feynman calculated that the work was done "nearly ten times as fast" after it had meaning.

Craft the Vision

Vision has the power to help people see the full impact of their work. Coaches can help leaders see the value of their work in several key areas.

1. *Spiritual growth.* Effective coaches model a life surrendered to Christ. The same is true for group leaders. Much of what leaders bring to group life is personal experience, maturity, and processes for growth.

2. *Giftedness.* As trust develops, coaches are able to help leaders gain an accurate picture of their gifts and abilities. What are their strengths? What are their growth edges? What is their God-given potential in leadership? What could God do through them and their group?

3. *Community.* Biblical community involves more than just small group meetings. Leaders will periodically need a reminder of the purpose of community—transformation, connected relationships, compassion, and mission.

4. *A leader's role in the church.* What is the church asking of leaders? What is their unique place in helping the church achieve the overall vision?

5. *Ministry multiplication.* Leaders seem to need constant encouragement and vision in this area. Leaders play a critical role in helping the church identify potential leaders, developing their skills and abilities (apprenticing), and multiplying the number of groups.

6. *Inclusivity.* All groups struggle at times with the challenges of adding new persons. Help leaders in your care regularly envision how to add new persons to their small groups at appropriate times and in appropriate ways.

(Tip: There is additional material on this subject in *Leading Life-Changing Small Groups*).

Clarify the Vision

It is important for coaches to help align each leader's vision for his or her group with the overall mission and vision for small groups in the church. For the most part, leaders do not look to their coach as the primary vision caster for the small group ministry; the small group pastor or director will often provide that vision. Instead leaders look to their coach for help to clarify and personalize the vision.

To move from the general vision and values of a church's small group ministry to the specific vision for a group or for a leadership gathering, coaches rely on the following:

Prayer. Often viewed as a last resort, prayer should instead be the first thing we turn to for help in clarifying and personalizing vision. "If any of you lacks wisdom, you should ask God, who gives generously to all without finding fault, and it will be given to you" (James 1:5).

Examination. Look closely at the issues. Prayerfully consider the strengths of your leaders, the challenges ahead, and the opportunities for growth. Gain a clear picture of reality.

Experience. Think about your leaders and your past experiences with them. What have you faced in the past that can shed light on future opportunities?

Innovation. Try to imagine new ways to tackle the challenges ahead. "Wise men and women are always learning, always listening for fresh insights" (Prov. 18:15 MSG).

When completed, the vision should paint a picture of what a leader is trying to accomplish in his or her group and in the lives of group members.

Keep the Vision Alive

It's one thing for your small group leaders to understand the vision for community in your church or the vision for how their small groups can change and grow. But for leaders to own the vision with enthusiasm and to translate it into action requires coaches to continually recast the vision. Why?

As odd as it sounds, leaders have lives. While they may be passionate about their small groups, they also have jobs, families, and other interests in life. Most are not thinking 24/7 about their small groups. Life can crowd out the vision.

Paul encouraged Titus to "remind the people" of Crete (Titus 3:1)—a prompting to all of us that vision "leaks." Unless you keep reminding your leaders of the vision, you may find they are wandering aimlessly with no clear sense of purpose or direction.

Here are some ideas to keep the vision alive.

Speak with clarity. If you can't articulate the vision clearly, odds are you don't understand and own it completely yourself.

Speak with conviction. When you talk about the vision, make sure your language is compelling, focused, and balanced.

Utilize every opportunity to clarify, cast, and recast the vision. Leadership gatherings, training events, group visits, conversations, emails, and phone calls are all prime opportunities to share key vision components or unpack an element of the vision. Be on the watch for opportunities to creatively connect the vision to common activities. For example, a conversation in the church lobby with someone new to your church is a great chance to emphasize to a leader the hunger for community.

Use Scripture. The Bible is filled with passages on community and with metaphors about doing life together in community. As you share with leaders, use these passages to support the vision for small groups.

Help leaders understand and own the church's vision. Provide time and a safe place for leaders to process what has been communicated to them about the vision and ask questions. This can be easily done in one-on-one conversations and in leadership gatherings.

Dream about the group and the possibilities for growth and outreach. Create space for leaders to dream and pray about God's desire for their groups. What is God calling their groups to do or be?

Help leaders break the larger vision into smaller, more manageable steps. For example, one of the first steps toward group multiplication (birthing) is to identify an apprentice leader. Who in each leader's group has the potential to be an apprentice?

Use stories that work. Watch for stories from leaders or groups that capture the heart of the vision in action in your church. Share these at leadership gatherings or in one-on-one conversations.

Celebrate when leaders achieve parts of the vision. Celebration communicates clearly to your leaders that what they are doing matters.

REFLECTION

Use the following chart to write the name of each group leader you coach. Write a sentence or two that describes their current vision for their group, as far as you can discern it now. (After you have discussions with your leaders, you'll be able to add to this.)

Group Leaders' Vision

1. _____:

2. _____:

3. _____:

4. _____:

5. _____:

Chapter 3

THE COACH'S TOOLBOX

A quick look inside the toolbox of a master carpenter will reveal his favorite tools. A well-worn tape measure, its markings faded. Wood chisels with sharp blades. A hammer whose handle fits his hand perfectly, shaped by years of use. A saw, a level, a square.

There are other tools there as well. These are highly specialized tools, used infrequently but still of great importance. When they are needed, he wields them with skill and precision. All of these tools, both the common and the highly specialized, are ultimately used for the same purpose: to transform nails, wood, and plaster into houses. He uses these tools to shape a vision and a plan into reality.

The same could be said of any person who daily works in a trade—a plumber, a landscaper, an architect, a machinist, or an engineer. Each of them has invested the time and energy to become skilled at using the tools of his or her trade, whether a wrench or a computer.

As we look inside the coach's toolbox, you'll discover a variety of available tools. Some you will use regularly. Some you will need rarely, if ever. Your success in transforming your vision for community and in developing the small group leaders in your care will depend on the level of skill and expertise you develop in using each of these tools.

Get to know them well. Invest the time to learn when and how to use each tool. These tools may feel awkward at first, the way a hammer felt the first time you tried to drive a nail. But over time, you will gain the skill and expertise to use them well.

THREE ESSENTIAL COACHING TOOLS

There are three primary tools you will use as you build into your leaders.

Each of these tools has a unique role to play in the balance of 3-D coaching. How to best utilize each tool will be explained in greater detail later.

1. *Coaching conversations.* A prayerful, planned conversation between you and a leader will prove to be the most often used and most valuable tool for you as a coach. Ralph Neighbour Jr. writes, "Nothing can substitute for personal time with each member of your flock! It will be in such private times that you will discern their value systems and deepest needs... there will be times when more private sessions will help you gain special insights into each person" *(The Shepherd's Guidebook).* These conversations provide a face-to-face opportunity to understand and meet the unique needs of each leader in a way that is not possible in core gatherings or group visits, whether those needs are about spiritual growth or concern an issue of group leadership.

2. *Leadership gatherings.* Leadership gatherings can be as simple as a single coach and his or her leaders getting together. They can be as large as an event involving a church's entire group life ministry. They can take place in a coffee shop, restaurant, home, church, or retreat center. Regardless of size or location, these settings provide the best opportunity to offer skill training to your leaders and to model a caring, nurturing community among the leaders. These gatherings of leaders and coaches are a perfect environment in which to cast vision and to celebrate when progress is made. While you might choose to emphasize one of these elements over another in a particular meeting, over the course of a year there should be a balance of all these elements in your core gatherings.

3. *Group visits.* Group visits allow you to observe firsthand the leadership skills and growth edges of your leaders. Observing a group in action will also give you a greater understanding of the specific, unique challenges and opportunities the leader is facing in that group. Every group is different! The insights you gain in the group visit will identify great topics to discuss when you have your next coaching conversation. Group visits also give you the chance to affirm your leader in the presence of the group.

Which Tool Should I Use First?

If you are a new coach, it's best to begin by building a relationship with each of your leaders. This is done most effectively in a one-on-one setting where you can have meaningful conversations. This coaching tool is the least intimidating to the leader. Depending on your personality type, you may also find that this tool is the one you are most comfortable using to nurture and develop your leaders.

As you build relationships, you can begin to visit the leaders' groups and design leadership gatherings for skill training and mutual support. Invest the majority of the first few gatherings in relationship building.

If you are an experienced coach and a new leader is added to your team, try to meet with that leader one-on-one as soon as possible. Getting to know you will make it easier for the leader to engage in existing relationships within your team. A visit to the new leader's group can come later, after the relationship is established.

TOOL 1: COACHING CONVERSATIONS

Imagine a conversation with a shepherd about the individual sheep in his flock. They may all look the same to you, but each of his sheep has unique needs and habits.

"See that one over there, the one with the ragged ear? It has a firm conviction that the grass *outside* the fence is better than the grass inside. So day after day he pushes his head through the barbed wire fence to nibble on forbidden delicacies. When he pulls his head back through the fence, he snags that right ear.

"See that lamb, the one struggling to walk? Her mother accidentally stepped on her when she was young. Broke her leg. Ewes are generally good mothers, but occasionally these things happen. The lamb is healing fine, but she'll walk with a limp the rest of her life."

Like a good shepherd, coaches know the leaders in their care. As you meet one-on-one with your leaders, you will learn more about their personal walk with Christ, their family life, and their deepest needs. You'll gain insights into the uniqueness of each leader — their strengths and weaknesses. These insights will help you nurture and develop your leaders. Nothing can substitute for personal time with them.

Think back to our young leader, Chad, whose story we encountered at the beginning of this book. What he valued deeply about his coaching relationship with Sean and Allison was that they cared about his leadership *and* his life. That came out clearly in the coaching conversations at the café. They talked about his spiritual growth, his relationship with his girlfriend, his work, *and how his group was going.* These coaches understood that life and leadership are integrated.

When Eric, Chad's newly assigned coach, was trying to build a relational bridge, the first step he took was to set up a coaching conversation with Chad. That proved to be a key decision. Their first conversation broke down a lot of Chad's resistance. Because of Eric's genuine interest and desire to build a relationship, Chad opened his heart that day, shared his story, and began a journey with his new coach.

Guidelines for Effective One-on-One Conversations

Build strong, healthy relationships with your leaders by following these basic principles.

1. Focus on relationship more than reporting. An easy assumption for any coach would be that the purpose of coaching conversations is to check in on leaders—to use the face-to-face time to make sure leaders are doing the right things. What curriculum are they using? Is life change happening in their group? Are they adding new people? Are they developing their apprentice?

These are important questions, and they often surface in these conversations. But a personal connection is what leaders most desire from their coach. It's the foundation of all your work with your leaders. One of the primary purposes of a coaching conversation is to help the coach establish a personal, pastoral relationship with the leader. This personal touch assures leaders that they are valued. It affirms both the leaders and their ministry. When coaching conversations are done well, leaders feel empowered and supported by their coach and the church. Leaders and coaches who stay together long-term are often able to develop deep and lasting friendships.

As you begin meeting one-on-one with leaders, your first steps will be to learn about their relational world (including family, friends, and work), their spiritual journey, and their leadership experience. Ask questions and listen deeply so you get to know each of your leaders well.

Over time, usually in just a few meetings, your conversations will begin to include developmental elements. Leaders will invite you into conversations about problems they are facing, new opportunities for growth or change. Within these conversations will be opportunities to explore God's dream for the leader and the group.

2. Focus on nurture more than skill development. Much of the time in coaching conversations is invested in nurturing the leader's soul, not developing their leadership abilities. A recent survey at our church affirmed this need. Leaders want their coach to be a shepherd first. They want you to *discover* their story, their group's story. Hear—or help them hear—what God is up to in their lives.

As the trust grows in your relationship, the leader will begin to share with you at a more personal level. Be patient; this may take time. They will open up about personal struggles or leadership challenges—issues they would not have shared with you at first. They may invite your input into struggles they are having as they lead their group. Only then can you move into *developing* the leader's abilities — addressing problems, challenges, and opportunities.

The depth of your relationship and the impact of your one-on-ones will increase over time if you do the following:

Listen intently. "Everyone should be quick to listen, slow to speak and slow to become angry" (James 1:19).

Strive for authenticity and openness through honest communication. "Speaking the truth in love, we will in all things grow up into him who is the head, that is, Christ" (Eph. 4:15).

Help them determine their next steps of growth. "[We pray this] so that you may live a life worthy of the Lord and may please him in every way: bearing fruit in every good work, growing in the knowledge of God" (Col. 1:10).

3. Focus on spiritual concerns more than organizational issues. Ministry growth strategies, reporting, and organizational charts should be saved for planning meetings. In coaching conversations, leaders rely on their coach for guidance and help with spiritual and personal issues. They desire to talk about the personal challenges of leading and loving their group.

Leaders are looking to their coaches to be caring, loving shepherds, not spiritual directors. Ask questions about your leaders' walk with Christ, their personal spiritual disciplines, and their participation in the life of the church. Pray for them and with them.

As you work to increase your leaders' spiritual depth, the quality of their leadership will improve.

4. Focus on encouragement more than management. Many leaders are apprehensive, even anxious, before their first meeting with a coach. They fear that the meeting will be less like a conversation with a friend and more like a trip to the vice principal's office. Communicate clearly to them before the meeting, and again as it begins, that you hope the time will be encouraging to them.

The apostle Paul's ministry provides a great example for coaches in the one-on-one meeting. He summarized his ministry to the church in Thessalonica this way: "With each of you we were like a father with his child, holding your hand, whispering encouragement, showing you step by step how to live well before God, who called us into his own kingdom, into this delightful life" (1 Thess. 2:11–12 MSG).

Other passages show just how important this ministry of personal encouragement was to Paul.

Acts 16:40. After being released from jail, Paul and Silas went to Lydia's house and encouraged the people meeting there.

Acts 20:1. After an uproar in Ephesus, Paul called the disciples together and encouraged them.

Acts 20:2. On his way from Ephesus to Greece, Paul stopped in churches and towns along the way and encouraged Christians.

Colossians 4:8. Paul sent Tychicus to the church at Colossae to encourage them.

What leaders need most from their coach is to feel supported and encouraged, not *managed*. Use encouraging words to help your leaders along in their spiritual walk. A good rule of thumb is a 5:1 ratio of encouragement to criticism, even if the criticism is constructive.

5. Focus on frequent connection more than high-impact conversations. We carry expectations into every relationship. They encompass needs, desires, hopes, and dreams. Leaders and coaches each carry their own expectations into any coaching relationship. Talking through these expectations will help define what will and will not happen in the relationship between coach and leader.

Schedule a regular meeting and make it a part of your ministry in your leaders' lives. The more frequent your meetings, the more quickly your relationships will deepen. In addition to having coaching conversations, stay in contact with each of your leaders through phone calls, emails, Facebook messages, and hallway conversations at church.

Notice we said *regular*. We did not say monthly or weekly, as though there were a one-size-fits-all approach to coaching conversations. How often you meet with a leader will depend on *their needs* and *mutual availability*. New leaders or leaders of groups in crisis will require more of your time. This may mean several contacts a week in order to help a leader navigate a conflict or to help a new leader through their first few group meetings.

Seasoned leaders will require less contact. Don't mistake that as a need for *no* contact or no coaching conversations. For this reason, it's a great step to ask such a leader to think through what care and support they would like to receive from you as a coach.

Take a few minutes now to use the reflection tool on page 70. Begin to think about the frequency and type of connection you will need to have with each of your leaders.

6. Focus on asking questions more than fixing problems. This is not just a coaching problem; it's a relationship problem that most of us struggle with. When we are involved in a conversation, our mind is typically not fully engaged in the art of listening. If we aren't distracted by our surroundings, then our minds have latched onto one or more details we heard in the conversation. Our thoughts are racing ahead to how we will respond when the other person has finished talking. More often than not in a coaching conversation, our response involves how we can help the person solve a perceived problem.

> The act of listening creates a great environment for change.
> — *Tony Stoltzfus,*
> Leadership Coaching

But the answer we offer is often misguided, simply because we didn't listen well. Proverbs is more blunt: "Answering before listening is both stupid and rude" (Prov. 18:13 MSG).

The better response when something piques your curiosity in a coaching conversation is to ask a question and then listen. Dig deeper into understanding the situation the leader is describing, the reaction of the group, what actions the leader took, and why. What are the leader's thoughts about it all? What leading has God provided about what to do next?

That simple act of listening and asking good questions will communicate to your leaders that you value them, you accept them. And if you listen intently and ask good questions over time? Your leaders will be more open to your ideas, thoughts, and influence.

REFLECTION

1. Think through any previous coaching relationships you have had. What was not helpful?

2. What are your expectations for your relationship with this leader in terms of how often you would like to meet? How long would you like those meetings to be?

3. What values (such as transparency, honesty, safety, confidentiality, and so on) do you feel are important to include in this coaching relationship? How will you talk about these with this leader?

4. How will you come to a consensus with this leader on what can and cannot be expected in this relationship?

How Do I Begin These Conversations?

Here are four simple steps to help you plan and lead a coaching conversation. The planning tool that follows these steps will help you implement them.

1. Pray

This step is easily overlooked. Spend time praying for and with each of your leaders. Paul said he prayed often and with great intensity for his leaders. In Philippians 1:3 – 11, Paul thanked God for his leaders in Philippi and for God's continued work in their lives. He prayed that God would give him the chance to be with them again, and he prayed for their personal walk, that their love for Christ might abound and that they might experience the fullness of Christ's righteousness.

Before each coaching conversation, pray that God will lead and guide the discussion. Ask him to show you areas where your leader needs to be affirmed, as well as those where he or she may need to be challenged or even comforted.

2. Prepare

Prepare for your meetings, considering in advance your conversation's focus and purpose. Good preparation will maximize your time with your leaders. Think through the following questions as you prepare.

1. What is your sense of how this leader is doing spiritually?
2. What one or two main issues would you like to discuss when you meet?
3. What issues from previous coaching conversations need follow-up?

4. Do you need to discuss any item from your last group visit or leadership gathering, such as a concern or a reason to offer praise?

It's also helpful for the leader to know what will be covered in the conversation, so that there are no surprises. Make a phone call or send an email to the leader a few days ahead of your meeting. Offer a summary of the main points of the upcoming conversation and encourage feedback. This will help alleviate any anxiety the leader may have about the meeting, as well as offer the leader a chance to prayerfully prepare for your conversation.

3. Personalize

As you meet with your leaders, keep the time personal. Each leader needs individual attention and care. Listen carefully to your leaders and offer feedback based on your observations. Help them evaluate their life and leadership so they will celebrate their strengths and continue to grow in their areas of weakness. Remember to speak the truth in love.

Before moving to your agenda for the time together, be flexible enough to respond to any issues your leaders are facing. There will always be time to cover essential agenda items; don't worry if you don't accomplish all your goals for every meeting. It's more important to deal with the conflict that happened in Sarah's group last week than to cast vision for her to find an apprentice. Better to listen and understand the family crisis that Bob is facing—to shepherd Bob—than to try to offer suggestions for improving the discussion level in his group meetings.

Work with your leaders to discover their strengths and their growth edges, in their spiritual life and in their leadership. Affirm their unique gifts and talents. Remember, each conversation always starts with *discover* before you move on to *develop* or *dream*.

Partner with your leaders in their overall development. Look for one or two practical things you can do to help them grow. Exchange ideas, key Bible verses, illustrations, and personal experiences that might help them toward their goals. Together develop specific action steps they can take before your next meeting (a book to read, a spiritual discipline to practice, a relationship to build, and so on).

4. Perspective

After each meeting (or series of meetings), gain insight and perspective by evaluating the time spent with a leader. Take a few minutes to record your thoughts so you can refer back to them before your next interaction with that leader. Use the questions in the "perspective" section of the tool below to help you in your evaluation.

COACH CONVERSATION PLANNING TOOL

Use this tool as a guideline to help you prepare for coaching conversations with your leaders.

Leader's name: _____

Date of conversation: _____

PRAYER

What can I be thankful for about this leader and his or her group?

In what do I sense this leader needs to be affirmed and encouraged:

challenged:

comforted:

PREPARE

Is there anything from previous conversations that needs follow-up?

List new ideas for the conversation, as best as you can discern in the leader's personal life:

spiritual life:

ministry to the group:

PERSONALIZE

To meet this leader's needs, which aspect of coaching does this conversation need to be more focused on?

PERSPECTIVE

1. In what ways did my leader feel heard, cared for, and supported?

2. In what tangible ways did I serve this leader?

3. Was the balance between *discover*, *develop*, and *dream* appropriate?

4. What issues need follow-up before our next meeting?

5. How did I utilize the teachable moments in the leader's life?

Development Aid: Coaching Conversations

The following guides focus on nine coaching conversations that are key to the success of small group leaders. The first guide is designed to help you with your initial conversation with a leader. The remaining guides are designed around eight key practices that are essential to a leader's growth and effectiveness. Those eight practices are:

1. Modeling personal growth
2. Shepherding your group
3. Building authentic relationships
4. Resolving conflict in a healthy manner
5. Extending care and compassion
6. Becoming an inclusive community
7. Reaching out to seekers
8. Developing future leaders

Here are some guidelines for effective use of these conversation guides.

1. Always begin each conversation by checking in. How is the leader doing personally? How is his or her group doing? A preplanned conversation should take place only if the leader's heart and head can receive it.
2. There are four main sections to each guide. The first relates to the coach's preparation through personal reflection; the others correspond to the three core practices of coaching.
   a. "Personal Reflection"—questions designed to help the coach prepare his or her heart and mind for the conversation.
   b. "Discover"—questions to help the coach understand the leader's journey and where the leader might need assistance or encouragement.
   c. "Dream"—information and questions to help the leader catch the purpose and value of this particular skill.
   d. "Develop"—additional training resources for the coach and/or leader.
3. As you review the conversation guides, choose the sections and questions that will be most helpful for your leader. Each guide contains enough questions for several meetings, so prayerfully consider which questions are best for this leader at this time. One or two well-worded questions will be enough for a one-hour conversation with most leaders.

(Special thanks to Mike Hurt. The coaching conversations he developed while at McLean Bible Church were immensely helpful in shaping these guides. Portions of those conversations are used here with his permission.)

CONVERSATION 1
Initial Conversation with a Leader

The Big Idea

To get past that initial, potentially awkward first conversation between a coach and a leader.

Select three to five of the questions from this guide, listen well to the answers the leader gives, and that should help you with a solid hour of conversation — and give you a good start to your coaching relationship!

Key Verses

- "The whole point of what we're urging is simply love — love uncontaminated by self-interest and counterfeit faith, a life open to God" (1 Tim. 1:5 MSG).
- "Encourage one another and build each other up, just as in fact you are doing" (1 Thess. 5:11).

Personal Reflection (for the coach)

As you prepare for this conversation, consider the following:

- What questions would you have if you were meeting your coach for the first time?
- What would you want most out of the first conversation?

The following questions are provided to stimulate your thinking and maximize your planning time. You won't need to use all of these questions; simply choose the ones that make sense for your meeting and shape them to fit your context.

Discover

Invite the leader to share about their family, their spiritual journey, and other aspects of their life.

- Are you married? Children? Other family in the church or in the area?
- How did you come into a relationship with Christ?
- How did you become a leader?

- What people have been influential in your life? How?
- What books have impacted your life? How?
- What have been the major turning points in your life?
- How did you come to be a part of this church?
- Where have you served in the church? How did those experiences impact you?

Develop

- What two things are going well in your group right now?
- Where are you seeing life change happen in your group?
- If you had a magic wand, what one issue or concern in your group would you resolve immediately?
- What issues or problems are you facing in your small group? How can I help you with these?
- What do you consider to be strengths in your leadership?
- Which skills would you most like to grow in?

Dream

- What are your hopes and dreams for your group?
- Who are you pouring your life into as an apprentice leader?

CONVERSATION 2
Modeling Personal Growth

The Big Idea

To help leaders follow God with increasing joy, humility, and gratitude so they are growing in the life of full devotion they are inviting others to live.

Key Verses

- "Follow my example, as I follow the example of Christ" (1 Cor. 11:1).
- "Not that I have already obtained all this, or have already been made perfect, but I press on to take hold of that for which Christ Jesus took hold of me" (Phil. 3:12 NIV 1984).
- "I consider everything a loss because of the surpassing worth of knowing Christ Jesus my Lord, for whose sake I have lost all things. I consider them garbage, that I may gain Christ" (Phil. 3:8).

Personal Reflection (for the coach)

As you prepare for this conversation, consider the following:

- What do you do to abide in Christ daily?
- What are some things that pull you away from Christ?
- Which of your experiences might help your leaders grow?

Discover

Invite the leader to share their spiritual journey with you. Listen intently and watch for key points of growth or struggle in their journey.

- What three people have most influenced your spiritual journey? How did they influence you?
- What books or authors have helped shape your walk with Christ?
- What issues or sins seem to be a recurring theme in your journey? How do you deal with these temptations?
- What spiritual disciplines or practices have been helpful in your growth to this point?
- Which disciplines are you able to practice on a regular basis?

Dream

Pressing on is a lifelong process. In Philippians 3:15, Paul challenges us to adopt his attitude. Pressing on is not always easy, but we must not give up. Persevering does not only mean facing obstacles; it also speaks of consistency, persistence, and a life of learning. To press on, we must learn how to continue growing in all stages of life. Each of us faces similar situations in our faith journey.

When we face exciting times of growth and God's activity. We wish all our times were like these. However, we need to be careful that we don't get spiritually lazy during these times.

- When did you last experience a time of exciting growth in your spiritual life?
- What do you think contributed to that growth?

When we face times of suffering and faith challenges. These are times we wish we could avoid. Tough times are fertile ground for spiritual growth. The key to continued growth during these times is to search for God's hand and purpose in the suffering or faith challenges.

- When is the last time you experienced a time of suffering or faith challenges?
- What helped you to see God's hand through your struggles?

When we face times of feeling distant from God. In the midst of these times, we long for God's activity in our lives. The key to continued growth during these times is to pursue God even if it seems he can't be found. Changing your routine can help refresh your walk with God.

- When was the last time you felt distant from God?
- What did you do to restore the closeness?

Develop

Disciplines such as prayer, Bible study, worship, giving, solitude, and accountability can help you pursue God.

- What spiritual exercises or disciplines would you like to develop to help in your walk with Christ?

- What experiences that have been helpful in your past (retreats, worship celebrations, serving opportunities) do you think God might be leading you to engage in again as a means of growth?
- What relationships in your life are helping you grow deeper with God and others?
- How can I assist you as you take your next steps of growth?

Resources you can recommend:

- *The Good and Beautiful Life* by James Bryan Smith, designed for individuals and groups, is a good study on spiritual growth and teaches spiritual disciplines.
- *The Me I Want to Be* by John Ortberg is a good life-application study.
- *Celebration of Discipline* by Richard Foster is a classic study in the spiritual disciplines.

CONVERSATION 3
Shepherding Your Group

The Big Idea

To help leaders listen and intentionally explore God's work in group members, in order to help members identify and take next steps of spiritual growth.

Key Verses

- "Their responsibility is to equip God's people to do his work and build up the church, the body of Christ. This will continue until we all come to such unity in our faith and knowledge of God's Son that we will be mature in the Lord, measuring up to the full and complete standard of Christ" (Eph. 4:12–13 NLT).
- "[We pray this] so that you may live a life worthy of the Lord and please him in every way: bearing fruit in every good work, growing in the knowledge of God" (Col. 1:10).
- "Grow in the grace and knowledge of our Lord and Savior Jesus Christ" (2 Peter 3:18).

Personal Reflection (for the coach)

As you prepare for this conversation, consider the following:

- In what ways have you provided this leader with an example of a shepherd?
- How can you better utilize your coaching conversations to shepherd the leader in his or her growth?

Discover

Allow the leader to reflect on their small group leadership. What components of shepherding are natural for them to employ with their flock? What components require intention and work? Depending on gifts and experience, shepherding may be challenging for this leader. The questions below will help you in this conversation.

- What steps have you taken to learn the spiritual journey of each of your group members?

- What signs are you seeing that would indicate that group members are growing spiritually?
- Where are group members in their spiritual journey? What issues are they struggling with?
- How are you encouraging the work that God is doing in your group members?
- What steps are you taking to lead group members to growth? (Encourage the leader to think of ways to help members grow in the time between meetings as well as in formal meeting times.)

Dream

For a fresh understanding of the shepherding heart of God, encourage the leader to review the following key passages. You may want to read and discuss them together.

Psalm 23
Ezekiel 34
John 10:1–21
John 21:15–19
1 Peter 5:1–4

- In these passages, what do you learn about God's heart for shepherding?
- Which areas of shepherding come naturally to you? Which ones do you need to work to develop?

Develop

Resources for making disciples and asking good questions can be found in *Leading Life-Changing Small Groups* and in *How People Grow* by Henry Cloud and John Townsend.

CONVERSATION 4
Building Authentic Relationships

The Big Idea

To help leaders maximize interaction in both formal and informal gatherings so that group members build authentic relationships in an environment of mutual accountability.

Key Verses

- "As iron sharpens iron, so a friend sharpens a friend" (Prov. 27:17 NLT).
- "Be devoted to one another in brotherly love. Honor one another above yourselves" (Rom. 12:10 NIV 1984).
- "Let the word of Christ dwell in you richly as you teach and admonish one another with all wisdom, and as you sing psalms, hymns and spiritual songs with gratitude in your hearts to God" (Col. 3:16 NIV 1984).
- "Let us consider how we may spur one another on toward love and good deeds" (Heb. 10:24).

Personal Reflection (for the coach)

As you prepare for this conversation, consider the following:

- How do you model openness and authenticity in coaching conversations with this leader?
- What activities or practices do you use to encourage authentic relationships in your leadership gatherings?
- Are there any behaviors you need to change (judging, criticizing, belittling, minimizing, inappropriate humor, and so on) to foster a deeper relationship with this leader?

Discover

Relationship building happens during the meeting time as well as between meetings. As you talk with the leader, help him or her think of ways to make the most of both opportunities.

During the Meeting

- How long have group members been together? How have they bonded?
- How would you describe the discussion and interaction in a typical meeting?
- How do you deal with people who may talk too little, too often, or too long?
- How would you like to see the discussions change or improve?

Between Meetings

- How do you stay in contact with group members between meetings?
- How do group members connect with one another between meetings (phone, email, coffee or meals together, trips, and so on)?
- What group activities, events, or retreats have you planned in addition to regular meetings?

Dream

If it would be helpful, offer examples of how other leaders have used the time between meetings to build relationships with and between group members.

Leaders can sometimes deepen the sharing and interaction in a group meeting by changing the type of curriculum used. Offer these simple ideas to help this leader.

Guidelines for Choosing a Good Study

- *Doctrinal purity.* Studies should be Christ-centered. Avoid topics that will polarize people within the group.
- *Relational in nature.* Every study must have a personal, sharing component.
- *Application oriented.* The goal is action and accountability, not just knowledge.
- *Sensitivity to needs.* Keep in mind the length of the group meeting, the amount of homework group members are willing to do, and their spiritual maturity.

Reflect on the following thoughts with your leader.

Community life is the place where our limitations, our fears and our egoism are revealed to us. We discover our poverty and our weaknesses, our inability to get along with some people, our mental and emotional blocks, our affective or sexual disturbances, our seemingly insatiable desires, our frustrations and jealousies, our hatred and our wish to destroy. While we are alone, we could believe we loved everyone. Now that we are with others, living with them all the time, we realize how incapable we are of loving, how much we deny to others, how closed in on ourselves we are. Community is the place where the power of the ego is revealed and where it is called to die so that people become one body and give much life.

— *Jean Vanier, Community and Growth*

CONVERSATION 5
Resolving Conflict in a Healthy Manner

The Big Idea

To help leaders create an environment where the truth is spoken in love, so group members experience reconciliation in their relationships with God and with other people.

Key Verses

- "All of you, live in harmony with one another; be sympathetic, love as brothers, be compassionate and humble. Do not repay evil with evil or insult with insult, but with blessing, because to this you were called so that you may inherit a blessing" (1 Peter 3:8–9 NIV 1984).
- "Patiently correct, rebuke, and encourage your people with good teaching" (2 Tim. 4:2 NLT).
- "Bear with each other and forgive one another if any of you has a grievance against someone. Forgive as the Lord forgave you" (Col. 3:13).
- "If a brother or sister sins, go and point out the fault, just between the two of you. If they listen to you, you have won them over" (Matt. 18:15).

Personal Reflection (for the coach)

As you prepare for this conversation, consider the following:

- What is your pattern for dealing with conflict in your life?
- What would you consider to be your strengths and weaknesses in this area?
- Is there any lingering or unresolved conflict or tension between you and this leader? What is your plan to resolve it?

Discover

- Ephesians 4:15 commands us to speak the truth in love. Which part of that is harder for you — speaking the truth or speaking in love? How does this impact your ability to engage in healthy conflict resolution?

- What do you understand to be the teaching from Scripture on how we are to resolve conflict in relationships?
- In your life, what is your natural pattern for conflict resolution? How does this line up with or differ from the teaching of Scripture?
- In what ways have you dealt with disagreements, hurt feelings, or broken relationships in your group?
- What tension or conflicts, if any, exist between members of your group right now?

Dream

Help the leader understand that conflict is normal and natural in group life. It will happen even in the best groups. As Larry Crabb says, "Conflict is latent in every human relationship at every moment. It simply awaits a trigger to get it going."

The Bible has a lot to say about how to handle interpersonal conflict. In addition to the verses listed above, the following passages provide helpful guidelines for leaders. Read one or more together and then reflect on the question below.

Matthew 18:15–17
Ephesians 4:26–27
Proverbs 15:23, 28
2 Timothy 2:24
Matthew 5:23–24
1 Corinthians 13
Proverbs 20:3
James 4:2

What would it be like for the group to resolve conflict in a healthy manner according to these passages? How would the group function differently than it does now?

Develop

Help the leader understand some of the root causes of conflict in group life.

- *Group stages.* In the early days of a small group, everyone thinks they love each other, because they really don't know each other. After a few meetings, the new begins to wear off. We start to see each other's wounds and washouts. Within six months or so, it's not uncommon for groups to experience their first conflict.

- *Relationally unaware group members.* A relationally unaware person seems to be either clueless or uncaring about interpersonal or group dynamics.
- *Needy group members.* This is someone who for very legitimate reasons needs a little extra love and attention from the group. Tension can come when these needs are chronic or long-term.
- *Interpersonal tension.* Sometimes people just rub each other the wrong way, and everyone can sense it. Usually the people involved are not trying to offend or be a pain. Sometimes personalities clash and friction develops between group members.

Resources that can help the leader grow in this area include:

- "Conflict Management" in chapter 5 of *Leading Life-Changing Small Groups.*
- "Care-Fronting: The Creative Way through Conflict" in chapter 5 of *Leading Life-Changing Small Groups.*
- "How to Have a Good Fight" in *Walking the Small Group Tightrope* by Bill Donahue and Russ Robinson
- *Caring Enough to Confront* by David Augsberger

CONVERSATION 6
Extending Care and Compassion

The Big Idea

To help leaders and groups offer tangible expressions of Christ's compassion as they care for people's needs personally and through the resources of the church.

Key Verses

- "If we don't love people we can see, how can we love God, whom we have not seen? And God himself has commanded that we must love not only him but our Christian brothers and sisters, too" (1 John 4:20–21 NLT).
- "Serve one another in love" (Gal. 5:13 NLT).
- "Carry each other's burdens" (Gal. 6:2).
- "Love one another deeply, from the heart" (1 Peter 1:22).
- "Each of you should use whatever gift you have received to serve others, as faithful stewards of God's grace in its various forms" (1 Peter 4:10).

Personal Reflection (for the coach)

As you prepare for this conversation, consider the following:

- In what ways have you extended care and compassion to your leaders?
- How might this leader need you to extend care or compassion in this conversation?
- What are some of the obstacles to caring for this leader? How can you overcome them?

Discover

- How do the members of your group care for one another as the body of Christ? (Invite the leader to share some recent examples. Watch for indications that the leader is encouraging the group to care for each other, in addition to personally caring for group members.)

- If your group struggles in this area, how might you guide them to more tangible expressions of Christ's compassion?
- How does the group balance Galatians 6:2 ("Carry each other's burdens") with Galatians 6:5 ("Each of you should carry your own load")?
- What needs exist in the group that may be beyond the members' ability to meet?

Dream

Spend time with the leader, reflecting on the following quotes from Scripture and Christian authors.

- "In this world you will have trouble" (Jesus, John 16:33).
- "Praise be to the God and Father of our Lord Jesus Christ, the Father of compassion and the God of all comfort, who comforts us in all our troubles, so that we can comfort those in any trouble with the comfort we ourselves receive from God" (Paul, 2 Cor. 1:3–4).
- "When life kicks us in the stomach, we want someone to be with us as we are, not as he or she wishes us to be. We don't want someone trying to make us feel better. That effort, no matter how well intended, creates a pressure that adds to our distress" (Larry Crabb, *Shattered Dreams*).
- "I feel helpless around people in pain. Helpless and guilty. I stand beside them, watching facial features contort and listening to their sighs and moans, deeply aware of the huge gulf between us. I cannot penetrate their suffering, I can only watch. Whatever I attempt to say seems weak and stiff, as if I'd memorized the lines for a school play" (Philip Yancey, *Where Is God When It Hurts?*).

1. How do these thoughts reflect your own feelings or experiences?
2. In what ways have you seen them to be true for members of your group?
3. What do you think are the next steps of growth for your group in terms of serving?

Develop

Resources that can help the leader grow in this area include:

- *Where Is God When It Hurts?* by Philip Yancey

- *Shattered Dreams* by Larry Crabb
- "Treating Wounds or Training Soldiers" in *Walking the Small Group Tightrope* by Bill Donahue and Russ Robinson (pp. 47–66)
- *The Five Love Languages* by Gary Chapman

CONVERSATION 7
Becoming an Inclusive Community

The Big Idea

To help leaders and their groups invite and include others so that everyone can experience community.

Key Verses

- "Accept one another, then, just as Christ accepted you, in order to bring praise to God" (Rom. 15:7).
- "I was a stranger, and you invited me into your home" (Matt. 25:35 NLT).

Personal Reflection (for the coach)

As you prepare for this conversation, consider the following:

- Think through groups you have led in the past. What were your struggles and successes in adding new people to them?
- How have you taught, modeled, and encouraged openness in the groups in your care?

Discover

- How has being in a small group affected your life? What if you had not been invited into this small group (or any other)? How would your life be different?
- What are the worst things that could happen if your small group invited someone new to be a part of it?
- What are the best things that could happen if your small group invited someone new to be a part of it?
- What struggles or opposition do you encounter within the group when you discuss adding a new person?
- Think through your last small group meeting. Did anything happen there that might make a new person feel uncomfortable?
- What changes need to be made to your current group so a new member would feel more welcome?

Dream

Spend time with the leader, reflecting on the following quotes from Scripture and Christian authors.

- "Go out and train everyone you meet, far and near, in this way of life, marking them by baptism in the threefold name: Father, Son, and Holy Spirit. Then instruct them in the practice of all I have commanded you. I'll be with you as you do this, day after day after day, right up to the end of the age" (Jesus, Matt. 28:19–20 MSG).

- "How can people call for help if they don't know who to trust? And how can they know who to trust if they haven't heard of the One who can be trusted? And how can they hear if nobody tells them? And how is anyone going to tell them, unless someone is sent to do it?" (Paul, Rom. 10:14–15 MSG).

- "A loving community is attractive. And a community which is attractive is by definition welcoming. Life brings new life.... Love can never be static. A human heart is either progressing or regressing. If it is not becoming more open, it is closing and withering spiritually. A community which refuses to welcome — whether through fear, weariness, insecurity, a desire to cling to comfort, or just because it is fed up with visitors — is dying spiritually" (Jean Vanier, *Community and Growth*).

- "The great enemy of community is exclusivity. Groups that exclude others because they are poor or doubters or divorced or sinners or of some other race or nationality are not communities: they are cliques — actually defensive bastions against community.... True communities, if they want to remain such, are always reaching to extend themselves. The burden of proof falls on exclusivity. Communities do not ask 'How can we justify taking this person in?' Instead the question is 'Is it at all justifiable to keep this person out?'" (Scott Peck, "The True Meaning of Community").

- "Show me a nurturing group not regularly open to new life, and I will guarantee that it's dying. If cells are units of redemption, then no one can button up the lifeboats and hang out a sign, 'You can't come in here.' The notion of group members shutting themselves off in order to accomplish discipleship is a scourge that will destroy any church's missionary mandate" (Carl George, *Prepare Your Church for the Future*).

1. What do these passages show you about the heart of God and inclusivity?
2. Where do these thoughts challenge your leadership and your group?

Develop

Resources that can help the leader grow in this area include:

- *Small Group Outreach: Turning Groups Inside Out* by Jeffrey Arnold
- *Missional Small Groups* by Scott Boren

CONVERSATION 8
Reaching Out to Seekers

The Big Idea

To help leaders and their groups develop relationships with seekers, understand their stories, and determine the best ways to impact those people with God's love so seekers can experience a personal relationship with Christ.

Key Verses

- "I will search for the lost and bring back the strays" (Ezek. 34:16).
- "Christ's love compels us, because we are convinced that one died for all, and therefore all died. And he died for all, that those who live should no longer live for themselves but for him who died for them and was raised again" (2 Cor. 5:14–15).
- "We are therefore Christ's ambassadors, as though God were making his appeal through us" (2 Cor. 5:20).
- "Go and make disciples of all nations, baptizing them in the name of the Father and of the Son and of the Holy Spirit, and teaching them to obey everything I have commanded you. And surely I am with you always, to the very end of the age" (Matt. 28:19–20).

Personal Reflection (for the coach)

As you prepare for this conversation, consider the following:

- Think carefully about your life and your evangelistic temperature. List the names of three people you know who are seekers or are not in a relationship with God.
- What steps are you taking to build a relationship with them?
- What are you doing to initiate spiritual conversations with them?
- How do your personal challenges in this area reflect the challenges your leaders may be facing?

Discover

- What does it mean to be an ambassador for Christ? How would our lives be different if we lived in such a way?

- How can we tell God's story to the world around us? What methods work for you?
- What roles do small groups play in sharing this message?
- How might your group react to the idea of inviting a seeker to join it?
- Think through your relationships with people at work, in your neighborhood, or within your family. Which of these people might be open to Christ or to community?
- When is the last time you reminded your group of the need to share Christ's love with the world?

Dream

Consider together these ideas for building the value of evangelism in the group.

Choose a Curriculum That Promotes Evangelism
- Do a study on grace.
- Study contemporary issues in evangelism.
- Study Jesus's reactions to various people groups.
- Continually apply the Bible to the world around us.

Lead Your Group in Service Projects
- Set the example in showing Christ's love to the world.
- Be consistent. Service projects are not reserved just for the holiday seasons.

Pray for Lost People by Name

An empty chair in the room can be a simple reminder to pray for people who don't know God.

Dialogue with the leader about what a seeker needs in a small group (Garry Poole, *Building Contagious Groups*):

- To be accepted where they are
- To be listened to and understood
- To be drawn out patiently
- To be cared for and served
- To be prayed for

- What next steps can you take as a leader to meet the needs of seekers?
- What next steps can you encourage group members to take?

Develop

Resources that can help the leader grow in this area include:

- *Seeker Small Groups* by Garry Poole
- *Small Group Outreach: Turning Groups Inside Out* by Jeffrey Arnold

CONVERSATION 9
Developing Future Leaders

The Big Idea

To help leaders develop a new generation of leaders so that Christ's redemptive purposes can be accomplished in our lives, in our groups, and in our community.

Key Verses

- "Pass on what you heard from me ... to reliable leaders who are competent to teach others" (2 Tim. 2:2 MSG).
- "It was [Christ] who gave some to be apostles, some to be prophets, some to be evangelists, and some to be pastors and teachers, to prepare God's people for works of service, so that the body of Christ may be built up until we all reach unity in the faith and in the knowledge of the Son of God and become mature, attaining to the whole measure of the fullness of Christ" (Eph. 4:11 – 13 NIV 1984).
- "As each part does its own special work, it helps the other parts grow, so that the whole body is healthy and growing and full of love" (Eph. 4:16 NLT).
- "He appointed twelve — designating them apostles — that they might be with him and that he might send them out to preach" (Mark 3:14 NIV 1984).

Personal Reflection (for the coach)

As you prepare for this conversation, consider the following:

- If your path into leadership involved serving as an apprentice, how did you benefit from that experience?
- Think of a group leader who has successfully developed and launched an apprentice leader. What principles and practices from this leader's story might be helpful to share with the leader you will be meeting with?
- How are you developing your apprentice coach? What successes and struggles are you experiencing?

Discover

- In what ways are you helping develop the gifts and abilities of members in your group?
- What tasks are you currently doing that you can give away to someone in your group?
- What steps have you taken to identify an apprentice leader in your group? What struggles have you had?
- What strengths, weaknesses, and motivations do you observe in your apprentice?
- What experiences, opportunities, and tasks are you using to develop the leadership and interpersonal skills of potential leaders in your group?
- How are you helping your apprentice grow spiritually?
- How are you using the time between meetings to develop your apprentice?

Dream

Examine the relationship between Jesus and the apostles in the Gospels. What did Jesus do to develop the apostles in all areas so they were ready to lead?

Spend time with your leaders, reflecting on the following quotes from Christian authors.

- "A man has truly begun to understand the meaning of life when he plants shade trees under which he knows he will never sit" (Elton Trueblood).
- "If I am to be someone's apprentice, there is one absolutely essential condition. I must be *with* that person. This is true of the student-teacher relationship in all generality. And it is precisely what it meant to follow Jesus when he was here in human form. To follow him, in the first place, meant to be with him" (Dallas Willard, *The Divine Conspiracy*).

If you were to live out the concepts described above, how would they impact your relationship with future leaders you are developing?

Develop

Resources that can help the leader grow in this area include:

- *Making Small Groups Work* by Henry Cloud and John Townsend
- *Developing the Leaders around You* by John Maxwell

TOOL 2: LEADERSHIP GATHERINGS

Imagine what it would be like to stand before an orchestra as its conductor. Seated in front of you are talented musicians, each with their own unique abilities and interests. The instruments they play are as varied as the people who hold them. You hear them warming up, and the sounds are disjointed.

As the conductor, your task is to blend all their talents, abilities, and knowledge into a coordinated effort. Following a musical score, you direct them to produce sounds in harmony with each other, resulting in beautiful music.

Planning a gathering for your leaders can be like conducting an orchestra. Each of them is unique; every leader has different talents and gifts. One may have years of leadership experience, while another is a brand-new leader. Each leader can play their own rendition of the music and lead a group with their own distinct style. All of these efforts will seem disjointed unless someone blends them together.

Coaches bring together all of this talent, ability, giftedness, and strength. You inspire the leaders to play together—to learn from you and from each other how to lead life-changing small groups. Just as the conductor follows a musical score, you follow a plan to develop your leaders. Together you learn from each other, support each other, and develop a team approach to ministry.

Scheduling Gatherings Is a Challenging Task

The pace of life has accelerated for most people, including group leaders. Our compulsive workaholism includes a longer workweek, compressed weekends and evenings, and unused vacation days. Our connection to technology (computers, smartphones, iPads) has made us accessible everywhere at any time. Our commitment to our kids and their development has us running nonstop to school and extracurricular activities, plus sports leagues run by the local athletic league or park district.

And it's often no easier for the empty nester. They are often caught between helping their married children get established in a new home and a new life and helping their parents face the challenges and illnesses that come with growing older.

If any of these things are true about your leaders' lives, imagine them getting an email from you or the ministry leader asking them to attend a leadership gathering. It often asks them to give up a half day or even a full day to come to a gathering to be developed.

For over twenty years, I was on the inviting side of this equation. I was the church staff member designing leadership gatherings and sending out the invitations. Then, by God's grace, I moved to a volunteer position in my church for six years. My eyes were opened to the difficult challenge of managing life, a more than full-time job, and a volunteer leadership position in a church. I began to understand *exactly why* leaders said no to the invitation to a leadership gathering.

Understanding this helped me get past the obstacles to effective leadership gatherings. If you are struggling in this area, you are not alone. It is a challenging task to craft leadership gatherings that bring value to a leader's life and ministry, honor their limited discretionary time, and speak directly to the needs of everyone in the room.

The Goal of Gatherings: Create a Learning Community

The goal of any gathering is to help establish a learning community. Those two words, *learning* and *community*, represent key components that coaches need to try to balance in their leadership gatherings.

Any time leaders are together, there is the opportunity to learn—not only from a trainer or presenter but also from each other. Leaders can catch a new vision for their group, learn a new leadership skill, or have their heart touched by a story of life change. If leaders are learning, your gatherings will have value. Over time, your leaders' interest in attending will remain strong.

Gatherings also offer the unique opportunity to build community with your leaders. Because leaders have a passion for building community, they often connect at a deep level when they are together. Encourage these connections by planning time in your gathering for the leaders to share experiences and to encourage each other. If the gathering itself does not allow the time for community, plan to go out for coffee or a meal afterward. If you build community into the event, leaders will have ownership and, again, their interest in participating will increase.

Biblical Examples of Leadership Gatherings

Several times in Scripture, we see groups of leaders gathered together in order to carry out effective ministry. Here are a few examples.

Mark 3. Following a time of ministry, Jesus withdrew from the crowds. As he often did, Jesus took the disciples away to be alone with him so that he could encourage and train them in ministry.

Luke 10. Jesus appointed and sent out seventy-two people into various towns to talk about the kingdom of God. Before they left, he commissioned them, trained them, and prayed for them. When they returned, he took them aside into another gathering time, where he listened to their stories, affirmed their efforts, focused their attention on the proper measurements for success, and offered a prayer of thanksgiving.

Acts 6. A disagreement arose in the church in Jerusalem. Though we are not given the details, it appears that the twelve apostles met privately to problem-solve before the final solution was announced. They called the church together to share a plan of action they had worked out together. The result was the selection of seven new servant leaders to take on significant ministry roles; new members were added to the leadership team.

Acts 15. Leaders came together in the Council at Jerusalem to problem-solve and make strategic decisions. There was a sharp disagreement among leaders, and it was in the context of a leadership gathering that the disagreement was resolved and the unity of the body preserved.

Five Reasons to Gather Your Leaders

Why have gatherings? Who needs more meetings? It's important to have clear and compelling reasons for gathering. Here are five.

1. To Learn

Work to create a safe environment where leaders feel the freedom to try, practice, and fail—all key components to good training. If leaders are learning, gatherings will have value, and over time leaders' interest in attending will grow.

Rather than thinking of yourself as a teacher or a trainer, consider ways to bring outside experts into your leadership gatherings.

> Find a three- to five-minute video clip from an online training site (or YouTube). Use it as a discussion starter for shared learning among your leaders.
>
> Select a small group resource to study together, such as *Making Small Groups Work* by Henry Cloud and John Townsend. Read a section of the book and discuss it together.
>
> Identify a common problem that most of the leaders are facing. Brainstorm possible solutions or next steps that leaders could take to resolve that problem. You could also do a role play with two or more leaders acting out the resolution of the problem.

Many churches offer centralized training for their small group leaders. Take advantage of these learning environments as a gathering time for your leaders. Encourage each of your leaders to attend, and then get together with your leaders to process what they've learned. How will their leadership change in the next thirty days based on what they have learned?

2. To Serve

Serving together with your leaders is a great way to build a deeper level of community and connection. For a number of years, I served with my coaches, leaders, and group members in the inner city of Chicago four times a year. Those serving times took us out of our comfort zone and our regular routine. They stretched us, presented us with unforeseen challenges, and helped us grow. They allowed us to see each other in a different environment and to see each other's strengths and weaknesses in a real-world application. Because if we're honest, it's one thing to talk about living for Jesus in our group studies; it's quite another thing to actually live for Jesus as we are serving the poor, the underresourced, and the marginalized in our society. Don't discount the value of a serving opportunity as a developmental gathering for your leaders.

> Find a local food pantry or homeless shelter and volunteer to serve for a morning.
>
> Check with organizations such as Habitat for Humanity, World Vision, or Compassion International or other organizations in your community to investigate ways you might serve.
>
> Talk with your church leaders to see if there are serving opportunities connected to your church that might be right for you and your leaders.

3. To Grow

Acknowledging that spiritual growth can be challenging, Dallas Willard said, " … all this appears to the ordinary Christian today like near or distant galaxies in the night sky: visible, somehow, but inaccessible in the conditions of life as we know them." Leaders can get stuck, both in their own growth and in how to lead their group for growth.

Leadership gatherings are not intended to replace a leader's personal walk with God or the growth that takes place in his or her group. But spiritual experiences offered in a leadership gathering can give group leaders fresh insights and new ideas for how to move forward. They can give leaders fresh wind in their sails so the leaders can help group members continue to pursue spiritual growth.

> Schedule a time of solitude (a half day or full day) at a local retreat center.
> With your leaders, attend a workshop, conference, or seminar focused on spiritual growth. If you can't attend, secure the audio file and listen to the workshop together and then discuss what you learned.
> Schedule time together with your leaders over a meal or coffee. Invite the leaders to come prepared to share what spiritual disciplines, experiences, or relationships have helped them grow the most.

4. To Relate

The principles of group dynamics apply to your leadership gatherings. Forming a strong relational bond between you and the leaders will make every aspect of coaching easier. Jesus said, "I am the good shepherd; I know my sheep and my sheep know me" (John 10:14), so schedule some time to be together with your leaders to get to know them. Make it a time that's convenient for them. And to uncomplicate life for them, try at times to make it a family gathering.

> Schedule a time with all of your leaders and their families. It can be a summer picnic, a fall trip to the apple orchard, or a casual dinner. Whatever you and your leaders would consider fun. Don't have an agenda other than simply being together.
> Invite one of your leaders to join you for a meal after church. Again, this is not a coaching conversation; there is no agenda other than getting to know the leader better.

5. To Celebrate

There are times when a party is necessary! Times when you and your leaders have completed a difficult task, resolved a challenging crisis, walked the family through a painful time. Those moments need to be marked and celebrated. It's a time to gather your leaders together and honor the work God has done in you and among you and through you. There were eleven separate celebrations commanded by God in the Old Testament Jewish law—celebrations that included huge amounts of food and good friends. I think that's a great pattern for us to follow with our leaders.

> There is a time for everything, and a season for every activity under heaven: ... a time to weep and a time to laugh, a time to mourn and a time to dance.
>
> — *Ecclesiastes 3:1, 4 (NIV 1984)*

Which of your leaders' accomplishments (in their life or in their group leadership) can you celebrate?

How can you celebrate the end of this ministry season?

Are there new groups launching, new leaders launching, or new leaders joining your team? If so, how can you celebrate these milestones?

Planning a Leadership Gathering

Each gathering that you plan will have a different emphasis. For example, one meeting might focus on relating, helping leaders get to know each other better and establish trusting relationships. Another might include an extended time of prayer, and yet another might train leaders in how to find and develop an apprentice leader. You will determine what to emphasize in each, based on the needs of your leaders.

Some needs may be obvious right away, but as you prayerfully consider the following questions, you will probably identify many areas of need. Remember, the overall purpose of coaching is to catalyze and encourage growth in your leaders. Here are some questions to consider as you prepare.

Discover

- What exercises or activities will help leaders discuss personal needs or struggles?
- What exercises or activities will help leaders discuss group leadership needs or struggles?
- How can I utilize this time to encourage leaders?
- What can we celebrate in leaders' group life and in their personal lives?

Develop

- With what leadership skills (relationship building, asking creative questions, listening, leading group prayer, and so on) do my leaders need help?

- What insights that would benefit my leaders have I gained from visiting groups and coaching conversations?
- How can I help my leaders learn from each other's experiences?
- What problems are my leaders encountering, and how can we work together to explore solutions?
- What information do my leaders need about future meetings, church-wide events, training opportunities, and updates?

Dream
- Can my leaders impart the vision for the small group ministry to their group members? How would they explain this vision?
- In what areas do my leaders need to be challenged or encouraged to dream bigger dreams?
- What ministry goals and expectations (developing an apprentice, adding new group members, and so on) need an update or accountability check-in?

Planning a gathering is like piecing together a puzzle. You won't be able to deal with every issue and every need in each meeting. So ask yourself, "What do my leaders need *most* from this time together?" Then plan accordingly. Remember to always ask your leaders what their needs are. It is an obvious but often overlooked question.

A Quick Test: Will This Gathering Have Value for Your Leaders?

After you plan your gathering, use this quick checklist to measure the value your meeting will have to your leaders. View the meeting through your leaders' eyes as they might be asking these questions.

- Is it worth my time and effort?
- Am I going to feel encouraged?
- Will it meet my needs?
- Will I learn something new?
- Will I have the opportunity to participate?

If your leaders can answer yes to these questions, you have planned well!

LEADERSHIP GATHERING PLANNING GUIDE

Gathering date: July 20   **Time:** 7:00 - 9:00 p.m.   **Place:** Andersons' house

PRAY

Spend time in prayer, asking God for insight and guidance as you plan.

I pray that the leaders will continue to have the willingness to add new people to their groups.

Pray for each of your leaders.

QUESTIONS TO CONSIDER

What are my leaders telling me?

They need ideas for getting members to pray out loud.

What do I need to ask them?

How is the Anderson group adjusting to the new couple?

What are my objectives for this meeting?

To build relationships, pray, and encourage spiritual growth.

Where is the Holy Spirit leading me?

To develop the relationships among the leaders.

Categories		Need/Issue	Time
Opening		Prayer and worship to begin.	15 min.
Discover	Community	Do a relationship-building exercise to encourage leaders to get to know one another.	30 min.
	Encouragement		
	Needs		
	Celebration	Andersons added new couple. Smiths' new apprentice.	10 min.
Develop	Skill training	Introduce creative ideas for group prayer.	30 min.
	Insights		
	Idea exchange	Invite leaders to share best/worst prayer ideas.	10 min.
	Problem solving		
Dream	Vision		
	Challenge		
	Encouragement		
	Goals		
Communication		New curriculum ideas. Fall leadership training at church	10 min

LEADERSHIP GATHERING PLANNING GUIDE

Gathering date: **Time:**   **Place:**

PRAY

Spend time in prayer, asking God for insight and guidance as you plan.

Pray for each of your leaders.

QUESTIONS TO CONSIDER

What are my leaders telling me?

What do I need to ask them?

What are my objectives for this meeting?

Where is the Holy Spirit leading me?

Categories		Need/Issue	Time
Opening			
Discover	Community		
	Encouragement		
	Needs		
	Celebration		
Develop	Skill training		
	Insights		
	Idea exchange		
	Problem solving		
Dream	Vision		
	Challenge		
	Encouragement		
	Goals		
Communication			

Leadership Gathering or Coaching Conversation?

At a leadership gathering, leaders should feel the freedom to share personal and leadership issues in safety. Set the tone that both successes and struggles are welcome. However, recognize that some issues are better dealt with in the one-on-one setting than in the gathering.

Here are some guidelines to help determine the best place to deal with issues that may arise in a leadership gathering. In all cases, be sensitive to the leading of the Holy Spirit when deciding how to handle each issue.

During the Leadership Gathering
- Never ignore or dismiss a need that someone brings to the gathering.
- Be an example of a caring leader.
- Encourage group leaders to support one another and help each other problem-solve.
- Allow leaders to ask questions and challenge each other.
- Encourage leaders to pray for each other during the gathering and between meetings.

At Another Time
- If the leader raises a personal issue, offer to discuss it at another time unless the person desires to discuss it with the other leaders.
- If there is a complex issue, one that would take a long time to resolve, schedule a different time to fully discuss it.
- If there is a unique situation to which no one else can relate, discuss it at another time.
- If confidences would be violated in any way, do not discuss the matter. Even the best leaders will at times have to fight the urge to share inappropriately. When leaders break the group's confidence (gossip), they teach other leaders that they can't be trusted. This will discourage deeper sharing in your gatherings.
- If you are not sure, wait until you know more about the issue to discuss it.

Developing Skills at Leadership Gatherings

Here are three steps you can take to maximize the gathering time for skill development.

1. Identify the Skill

Coaching conversations and group visits will help you assess which skills need to be developed or improved in your leaders. Some skills to focus on might be:

- Effectively using icebreaker questions
- Doing relationship-building exercises
- Using the Bible effectively in groups
- Listening well
- Writing and asking good questions
- Leading group prayer
- Dealing with talkative or shy members
- Choosing and using curriculum
- Managing group dynamics

2. Model the Skill
- Try out new leadership practices or techniques in the meeting.
- Adults learn best by doing. Don't just teach the skill; give leaders a chance to try it for themselves.
- After leaders have experimented with these skills in the meeting, encourage them to take the ideas and methods back to their group.

3. Involve Others
- If there is a leader who is strong in a given skill, invite them to help train the other leaders. For example, if someone has done creative things with prayer in their small group, ask them to use their ideas to lead a prayer time as an example for your leaders.
- As a coach, you will not have experienced everything your leaders will face in their groups. Nor will you be strong in every skill your leaders need. If you encourage leaders to share experiences and ideas, they will learn to value each other and ask one another for help with problems.

Evaluating Leadership Gatherings

As soon as possible after your gathering, take a few minutes to answer the questions below. They will help you evaluate the effectiveness of your meeting and will assist you as you plan your next one. If you have an apprentice coach, evaluate together. You may also want to invite the leaders to share their evaluations.

- What went well? What did not go well?
- Was there enough time for each exercise or activity?
- How could the experience be improved?
- How did the gathering help build community with the leaders?
- Did the leaders feel encouraged?
- Did the time have value for the leaders?
- What items need follow-up?

Development Aid: Leadership Gatherings

The following guides for leadership gatherings are designed around the eight key practices that we believe are essential to a small group leader's growth and effectiveness. Here are the eight practices again to refresh your memory.

1. Modeling personal growth
2. Shepherding your group
3. Building authentic relationships
4. Resolving conflict in a healthy manner
5. Extending care and compassion
6. Becoming an inclusive community
7. Reaching out to seekers
8. Developing future leaders

For your reference, we have included some common components for each gathering you lead. Obviously, leadership gatherings will not all look the same and should never have a regimented or mechanical feel. We give you a framework to help you organize and develop them. Gatherings shouldn't be predictable or routine. Exercise creativity by varying the order of and time spent on each segment of your gathering.

These guides can be adapted and used in many settings — with one coach and his or her leaders or in a larger ministry setting.

Each guide is designed to help coaches utilize some or all of the three core practices of 3-D coaching: discover, develop, and dream. When helpful, there is also an opening exercise for community building.

Open. A time for building community and checking in personally. This can help set the tone and help leaders develop relationships. Remember that leaders see your life and may follow your example — or lack thereof.

Discover. Help leaders grow spiritually by reading Scripture together, sharing stories with one another, and asking them questions about how God is at work in their lives and in their leadership.

Develop. Work together to solve problems, develop creative ideas, share experiences, and brainstorm for the future direction of the ministry. This may also involve skill training or connecting leaders to resources that will help them become more effective.

Dream. This may include prayer, storytelling, and worship so that God is recognized as the source of all ministry growth. It involves pointing to the future and reminding each other that God will continue to do his work through us by his grace.

GATHERING 1
Modeling Personal Growth

Focus: To help your small group leaders model a Christian life that is characterized by the ways and teachings of Jesus Christ.

Key passage: 1 Timothy 4:11–16.

Goal: To guide leaders through a spiritual inventory that enables them to "pay close attention to themselves," as Paul exhorts Timothy to do.

Materials needed: Paper and Bibles.

Logistics: Consider serving refreshments, and if possible, choose a place that allows for some quiet reflection.

Open

- Begin your time with prayer, and guide your leaders into a time of thankfulness and expectation for your time together. Ask God to help your minds slow down and focus on the time you have as a leadership community.

- Take about ten minutes to discuss the period of time since your last contact. Ask leaders for brief, personal updates — how they are doing on a scale of one to five, with five meaning strong and energized, and one meaning depleted or tired.

- Ask a few opening questions: What does it mean to be an example to others of the spiritual life that a person should lead? Is it overwhelming? Intimidating? In light of how each leader is doing, is this an impossible task? Do leaders understand that the power of Christ is revealed through us, that we are only clay jars? Remind leaders that they are examples in success and in failure. We do not hide our failures; we let Christ redeem them for growth in our lives.

- Read 1 Timothy 4:11–16 and discuss the implications of the passage. Note that Paul emphasizes both the opportunity and the obligation Timothy has as a leader.

Discover

Look at the areas Paul listed in verse 12 and use them as a kind of spiritual inventory. Ask leaders to examine their lives in each area:

speech, conduct, love, faith, and purity. If they could develop in one area over the next thirty days, what might that be? How are these areas integrated?

> *Speech:* how I use words
> *Conduct:* how I face trials and decisions
> *Love:* how I engage in relationships
> *Faith:* how I trust Christ for strength and connect with him
> *Purity:* how I face my sin and grow in character

Spend time encouraging one another to pursue a life like Christ's with an attitude of surrender. Remind leaders that they are not perfect and that we all need to come before God each day and renew our commitment to him, confessing sin and asking for strength and power for the day ahead. Remind them that the Holy Spirit is at work. Show leaders what you are doing to follow Christ, how you come to him for strength, and that you also need his healing grace.

Dream

Take a few minutes to tell your leaders how their intentional pursuit of character growth and purity will have a ripple effect on their small group members. Look again at 1 Timothy 4:16, where it's clear that Timothy's work will not only have a personal benefit (save him from a life of sin and disobedience) but also benefit others (save them from living in ways that destroy them spiritually and hurt the church in Ephesus).

Joe Stowell told a group of small group leaders years ago, "It takes a changing life to change a life." You might read this to your leaders and encourage them to be the kind of person who has a changing life.

Develop

Recommend the spiritual discipline of periodical self-examination and peer examination. For self-examination, leaders can simply have a regular quiet time for reflection, in which they ask the Spirit to point out areas of weakness as well as areas of strength. For peer examination, encourage leaders to have a "spiritual friendship" with someone they trust who can speak into their life, giving them feedback about their character, attitude, behavior patterns, spiritual gifts, and development as a leader. A mentor would be an ideal person for this.

Also recommend some additional reading such as *Spiritual Leadership* by J. Oswald Sanders, which focuses on the character and practices of a Christ-honoring leader.

A great Bible passage to read and reflect on is John 15:1 – 17.

GATHERING 2
Shepherding Your Group

Focus: To help leaders feel comfortable with their role as a spiritual guide in the life of others.

Key passage: Matthew 22:34–40.

Goal: To provide leaders with a simple way to guide others into a deeper relationship with Christ.

Materials needed: Paper and Bibles.

Logistics: Consider meeting in a place where leaders can sit around tables or in a circle for better group discussion.

Open

- Connect for a few minutes with some refreshments and catch up on one another's week. Make this time light and informal to set a relaxed and less structured tone.
- Pray for leaders in your group by name. Call out to God on behalf of or with each one, based on the needs and strengths they have. In this way, you will model how to pray specifically for people at a small group meeting. It is powerful to pray for someone in the presence of others, and it shows your knowledge of their lives, your interest in their needs, and your passion for their growth and success.

Discover

- First, gather your leaders into a circle and ask them to read Matthew 28:19–20. Since we are to obey all that Jesus commanded his followers to do, have them list as many of Jesus's commandments as possible. (There are several hundred, but we want to show them that Jesus boiled down all his commands to two.)
- Now ask leaders to read Matthew 22:34–40. What is the focus of all of Jesus's commands?
- *Group discussion.* Ask leaders to share together for a few moments around these questions: How do you feel about being a spiritual guide, moving people forward in their relationship with Christ? Do you feel inadequate? Excited? Nervous? Grateful?

Dream

Help leaders see that guiding people is simple, in that it all comes down to loving God and loving others. Encourage leaders to remember this. It's all about relationships, both with God and with other people. That is why their small group ministry is so essential. It has a strong focus on relational health, helping their members grow in their relationships with God and with other members, as well as with people outside the group (friends, family members, fellow believers in the church, and so on).

Develop

Leaders might want to have this same "love God, love others" discussion with their small groups. Here's a way to help them do that.

Question for a small group: What does it look like to love God? To love others?

Give the small group a simple exercise for this discussion. Go to Exodus 20:1–17 (the Ten Commandments) and ask members to divide the commandments into the two categories below.

1. Love to God
2. Love to others

Then, as a small group, discuss how the members *together* can help one another become more loving. Describe practical ways to express love to God and love to other people.

GATHERING 3
Building Authentic Relationships

Focus: To give leaders the confidence to guide discussions.

Key passages: Proverbs 17:27–28; 18:13.

Goal: To equip leaders to create an environment that promotes discussion in their groups.

Materials needed: DVD player or computer, Bibles.

Logistics: Some snacks and a room in which to watch the movie clip.

(*Note to coaches:* Choose a four- to six-minute clip from a movie or a TV show that portrays a group discussion or argument. The discussion could be a great one, or it could be a poor one in which people interrupt and don't listen well. It doesn't matter. But the more interaction, the better. Use discretion regarding language, content, movie rating, and so on. No need to create unnecessary conflict or distract from the point of the meeting.)

Spend a few minutes to greet each other and connect relationally. Keep this brief unless there is a crisis to deal with.

Dream

Begin this session with some vision casting. Ask, "What would it look like to have a group discussion flow so well that you, the leader, could leave the room for twenty minutes and when you return, the discussion is still going on and no one knows you ever left? What would the elements of such a discussion be?"

Take a few minutes to list responses on paper.

Develop

- Show the clip from the movie or TV show and ask leaders if they see anything they listed (qualities of a good discussion) in the clip. What are the communication patterns like? How would they lead this discussion if it were a meeting? What role does listening play?
- Read Proverbs 17:27–28 and Proverbs 18:13. What key to facilitation is taught in these verses?

- What does it feel like to be listened to and *really* heard? How do we know that we have been heard and understood?

As you lead this discussion as a coach, make sure you model good listening skills. Ask good questions. Show genuine interest. Use phrases like "Tell us more about that" and "Why do you feel so strongly about that?" Listen to body language and people's tone of voice. Watch their energy level as they talk. Observe who talks the most. Consider how to draw others into the conversation. "Sarah, would you add anything to what has been said so far?"

If you want to have some fun, model poor listening skills. Interrupt people. Nod a lot and say, "Uh-huh" but ask no follow-up questions. Change the subject quickly, and then spend more time talking about your own feelings and experiences. After a while, stop the meeting and ask leaders what they observed about what you just did. Ask if they do this in groups, becoming so focused on the agenda that they can't really listen to the feelings, interests, and words of members.

- Recommend the "Listening Skills" section in chapter 2 of *Leading Life-Changing Small Groups* as a guide. It compares active listening versus passive listening, and the results of each.
- Take a few minutes to have leaders simply practice listening and asking good follow-up questions. Ask someone to be the observer and give feedback to leaders after this exercise. Have some fun with this.
- Remind leaders to pay attention to what is happening in the circle when there is a discussion going on. Who is talking? Who is getting ignored? Who feels scared? Who needs encouragement? What kinds of questions are being asked? Remember that closed questions (questions that have right and wrong answers or are questions of "fact") will not generate much discussion. Open questions (questions of feeling, opinions, reactions, ideas) invite people to talk and express their thoughts and open their hearts.

GATHERING 4
Resolving Conflict in a Healthy Manner

Focus: To address conflict and help people speak the truth in love.

Key passages: Matthew 18:15–18; Ephesians 4:25–32.

Goal: To equip leaders to engage in conflict as it arises and to face conflict with grace and truth.

Materials needed: Bibles and some three-by-five-inch cards or paper.

Logistics: Contact one of your leaders ahead of time and ask them to bring a case study of a conflict situation, either in personal life or in group life. No names. Make sure confidentiality is honored. Debrief this with them before asking them to bring it to the group. Ask them to limit their example to one page, to type it if possible, and to have copies for the group. If this isn't appropriate, create a case study yourself. The case should include a brief statement of the situation, the background of the conflict, and the process that took place. Include the reactions and responses of people involved. Do not describe the resolution yet. Just describe the tension and the problem. In your meeting, you will explore solutions and then see what really happened.

Discover

Begin with sharing a story of a relational breakdown in your life (not your case study if you are bringing one to the gathering). This could involve a conflict at work, a friendship while growing up, or a family situation. Describe how you dealt with it, where you failed in addressing the conflict appropriately, and what you did well. Stories are great ways to encourage others, to show your own failures and humility, and to model for leaders the practice of storytelling.

As you do this, you also model appropriate self-disclosure and confidentiality (how you describe the conflict without embarrassing the people involved or violating their confidence).

Pray that each leader would have the courage to face the challenging aspects of group life as conflicts arise or as difficult people enter a group and create tension.

Develop

- Hand each leader a three-by-five-inch card and ask them to write down what they believe is the key to facing relational tension in groups. What is important to do and not to do? Collect the cards and see if, as a group, you can prioritize what they have shared.
- Check the list against Ephesians 4:25–32 and the process of Matthew 18:15–18.
- Now distribute the case study and have leaders, in groups of two to three, discuss the situation and see what they would do. After talking about the case, read the results of what happened. Was the conflict resolved? Is it still being worked on? What's at stake? How do the participants feel now? Is there complete reconciliation? If not, why? If so, what made this happen?

Dream

Help leaders see that conflict can be met with grace and truth. We speak in love to one another but do not hold back truth. We courageously face the relational breakdowns that threaten our oneness in Christ (John 17:20–23) and the health of our groups. Encourage your leaders to have hope — many conflicts work out over time with the right biblical process and attitude. But some do not, and we need to be prepared to work through that result as well, regardless of whether it involves the whole process of Matthew 18:15–18.

- Encourage leaders to not fear conflict but fear avoiding it when it should be dealt with. Running away from conflict will destroy a group or a relationship.
- Lead everyone in a time of prayer. Ask leaders to write the names of people in their group or in their life whom they must meet with to begin the process of healthy conflict resolution. Remind leaders that they model to their group members how to handle conflict. If they don't honor the biblical process, the group will see this and probably ignore the process as well.
- Ask leaders to speak with their groups, asking members to evaluate (individually or collectively) how well the group is doing in facing tension when it arises. What steps could members take to improve the way they handle relational challenges? Who needs to extend forgiveness?

GATHERING 5
Extending Care and Compassion

Focus: To discover creative ways to grow the servant hearts of leaders.

Key passage: Matthew 9:35–38.

Goal: To help leaders identify serving opportunities and evaluate their hearts, and the hearts of their group members, for compassion.

Materials needed: News magazines.

Logistics: Consider having your gathering at a place where there is great need in your community.

Open

- Begin with a time of prayer for people in need of help and compassion. Ask leaders to name friends, family members, and others in their lives who require prayer for social, physical, and financial help.
- Read Matthew 9:35–38 and ask, "What is the focus of the shepherds Jesus is looking for?"

Dream

- Ask members to look through magazines and cut out photos that show people in need — the poor, the hungry, refugees, orphans, war victims, and so on.
- What do you feel when you see these photos? What happens to your heart? How does your heart connect with Jesus's heart as he looked over Jerusalem?
- What would it look like if our churches and our small groups could reach out and meet some of the world's needs? What kinds of needs can be addressed right in our own neighborhoods or near our church? What might that look like?

Develop

Take some extended time to help leaders evaluate the gifts and passions of group members and the needs in their communities.

1. My group members' gifts and passions:

2. Community needs:

3. Our opportunities:

Ask leaders to spend a few minutes on this alone, then gather your leaders together to find out what each one sees as opportunities their group could act on. What are the common needs? How could groups come together to meet these needs? How could your gathering of leaders act collectively to meet the needs in a community, mobilizing all of their groups toward the same end?

Read Matthew 25:31–46 to understand how important this is to Christ.

Discover

This is an opportunity for us as coaches to lead the way, to show our heart of compassion for the poor, lost, lonely, and needy folks in our churches and neighborhoods. Describe how you are praying for these people, reaching out with your family, giving of your time and resources to help others. Not in a prideful way but to show your leaders that you believe in the cause and are acting on it.

GATHERING 6
Becoming an Inclusive Community

Focus: To help develop the practice of inclusion, encouraging leaders to open their groups to people different from themselves.

Key passage: Psalm 67.

Goal: To help leaders and their groups identify ways of becoming more inclusive.

Materials needed: DVD.

Logistics: A place to watch a movie.

Dream

After some brief checking in and snacks, consider watching a movie that reinforces the need for inclusion or that emphasizes racial reconciliation, the overcoming of oppression, or class struggles. Recommended movies would be *Gandhi* (about India), *Invictus* (about South Africa), and *Michael Collins* (about Ireland), or you might have another one in mind. If you can't take the time to show an entire movie, show a lengthy clip that is powerful. Twenty to thirty minutes is good.

- Debrief the film. What motivated the people to fight against injustice and seek to be included? How might it feel to be on the outside looking in?

- Take time to pray for a heart for people of other races, creeds, colors, and experiences. Ask God to open wide the hearts of your small group leaders so they can begin to model this inclusion for their groups.

- Read Psalm 67. Even though Israel was God's chosen people, what is the heart of God for the nations? How can we develop such a heart? What other materials (such as the book *Divided by Faith* by Michael O. Emerson and Christian Smith) can we read to understand the plight of people who are not part of the power structure of our country?

Develop

- Spend time brainstorming what inclusivity would look like in the small groups represented here. What does it take to open our groups? How do we build personal relationships that model this openness?

- Invite someone from a different faith, race, background, or viewpoint to come to your gathering. Interview them. What's important to them? How can a church help them? What would they want us to know about them? About others like them?

- What is the church already doing that your small groups can connect to so that people's hearts for inclusivity grow?

Discover

Begin to pray for and develop relationships yourself. List some people you could get to know better at work or in the community. It may be a businessperson or a single parent or a missionary on furlough who has experiences in other cultures.

GATHERING 7
Reaching Out to Seekers

Focus: To help leaders gain a heart for the lost and help their groups develop the same.

Key passages: Ezekiel 34:16; Luke 15.

Goal: To inspire leaders and their groups to pray for and connect with opportunities to reach people who are far from God.

Materials needed: Paper and Bibles.

Logistics: Consider inviting a non-Christian friend to come to your meeting during the snack or meal time. During this time, ask them to describe their understanding of God and their view of Christians. After the friend leaves, have your meeting and discuss their comments.

Discover

Describe the relationships you are developing with non-Christians and what priority they have in your life. If this is an area of weakness for you, simply admit that and make a commitment to improve. Ask your leaders for accountability and prayer as you move ahead. List the names of people you love and care for who do not know God, and ask leaders to do the same. Using only first names, pray for these people.

- Read Luke 15 and ask your group leaders what they notice about the three parables. What is Jesus trying to show us about the heart of the Father toward people who are strays, wandering from him?
- What is your leaders' attitude toward people who are far from God?
- If you invited a non-Christian for dinner, what did they say? How do you feel toward them?

Dream

Remind leaders that within two years of becoming a Christian, most believers lose all significant contact with the unchurched and have no close unchurched friends. How can we remedy this?

What would it look like if each small group would befriend two people over the next year, build a relationship with them, invite them to social outings, and invite them to church? What impact might that have? What if each member of each small group did that? You could impact forty to fifty people!

Develop

- Encourage members to take an evangelism training course like *Becoming a Contagious Christian* so they will know how to build relationships and share their faith with lost people in an intentional but not oppressive way.
- Take a few moments to share ways to start spiritual conversations with people. Consider inviting someone who works regularly with lost people to come to your next gathering or to visit leaders' groups to share their stories and vision.
- Consider reading a brief book together as a small group to help people catch a vision for seekers and to build a relationship with people they already know who are not connected to Christ.

GATHERING 8
Developing Future Leaders

Focus: To help leaders see that the ministry continues when we invest in others toward leadership.

Key passages: Mark 3:14; 2 Timothy 2:2.

Goal: To help leaders identify potential leaders in their group and begin building into them.

Materials needed: Paper and Bibles.

Logistics: A simple meeting room or a home, refreshments.

Discover

- As a coach, describe for your leaders a time when someone built into you. What was the effect? Is that person still a mentor today?
- Ask leaders to describe a time when someone built into them.
- Describe what you look for in an apprentice, someone you would invest time in.

Dream

- What would happen in our church if every existing small group leader identified and built into just one person in the coming year? If that one person became a leader, how many new groups would that generate? How many people would now have an opportunity to experience group life?
- If you have an apprentice, bring the apprentice to the gathering. Let leaders meet and interact with the person (or people) you are developing.
- Help leaders see that they can invite others to grow into leadership instead of jumping into it right away. Becoming a leader is a process, and there is time to grow under the supervision and encouragement of others who are leading now.

Develop

- Find a leader in your church who is good at developing others, whether they do that in the church or in their workplace.

Interview them. What do they look for? How do they start? What should we be careful of when inviting others into leadership?

- Spend time creating a list of potential leaders in your church. Now list the obstacles that are keeping them from leading. Is it a lack of skills, training, or vision? Is it a negative experience or fear? Brainstorm ways to address those obstacles.

- Consider bringing a formerly reluctant leader to the gathering or to a training session for leaders at the church. Ask the person what helped them take the plunge into leadership. Who helped them?

- Read 2 Timothy 2:2 and Mark 3:14. What do you notice about what Jesus did and what Paul did? You might also look at Matthew 10 and Luke 10, where Jesus gave people on-the-job training as leaders.

- Pray for spiritual eyes to see potential leaders (they often don't look like leaders) and for the courage to boldly ask those people to enter a development process, a partnership. Ask them to join a leadership community by attending your gathering, so they can see what leaders do. Invite them to a small group meeting.

- Help your leaders see this as a spiritual battle. Matthew 9:35 – 38 says we need to pray for workers in the harvest. God must move in their hearts, and the Evil One hates leaders — because they start little communities called small groups that can change the world. So pray!

TOOL 3: GROUP VISITS

Each day, physicians in hospitals around the globe make rounds, checking on patients under their care. They visit these patients to assess their condition, provide information and encouragement, and make suggestions for improvement. They show care to everyone they visit, paying attention to each patient's general well-being.

Likewise, coaches are called upon to make the rounds, visiting each group, paying attention to the well-being of the leader and the members. Coaches provide care and try to correct any health problems that may exist. They give information as to what practical steps can be taken to grow a healthy group.

If done correctly, a coach's visit should leave the group members and the leader feeling encouraged. They will be glad the coach came and will look forward to the next visit. That's the mark of a good shepherd—and a great coach.

The Purpose of Group Visits

In Acts 15:36, Paul and Barnabas decided to go to every city where they had preached the gospel. Their desire was to encourage the churches, to see how they were doing, and to offer any assistance needed. Like Paul and Barnabas, coaches visit groups to see what is being done, to confront any problems, to encourage the leaders and members, and to help groups grow.

You can easily discover the basic facts about a group—such as what curriculum is being used, who the group members are, who is leading, and when and where the group meets—without ever personally visiting. Drop in on a typical group meeting, and you will gain insight into some of the intangibles, such as the following:

- Are healthy, authentic relationships developing in the group?
- Is there any unhealthy conflict in the group?
- Are group members growing spiritually?
- Is the group welcoming new people and including them in all of group life?
- How is the leader utilizing and developing the gifts of group members?

Keys to Effective Group Visits

An effective group visit will provide support and encouragement to the leader as well as to the members. To maximize your visit, consider the following measures a coach can take to meet the group's needs.

Calm the Leader's Fears

Leaders may have some anxiety about your visit. This is almost always true for the first visit, but hopefully the anxiety will subside after that. Members may also have questions about why you are coming to check out the group.

REFLECTION

Take a moment to list the fears your leaders might have when you mention that you would like to drop by and visit their group. How can you help alleviate those fears?

For this reason, it's good to establish a relationship with the leader before visiting the group. Leaders need to know they are important to you, not just because of the ministry successes they are having but also because of who they are.

Leaders also need to know that you are there to help them. Assure them that your purpose in visiting their group is to support and encourage them, to be a resource, and to provide ideas for the group. You are *not* there to criticize them or point out things they're doing wrong.

While there is accountability involved, the leader shouldn't fear your visit, because your main objectives are to be a mentor and to develop leadership skills.

Be an Encourager

The apostle Paul spent a great deal of his ministry encouraging other leaders and Christ followers. He so highly valued encouragement that when he could not go personally, he sent Timothy, Silas, or another representative, with the primary purpose of encouraging people.

Your leaders need encouragement. Even the most seasoned, successful leaders experience times of discouragement; some may even feel like quitting. Leaders often have no idea of the difference their leadership is making in people's lives.

Your group visit will be an encouragement if you do the following:

- Use the 10:2 rule—provide ten encouraging comments for every two suggestions for improvement.
- Tell group members how much you appreciate their leader. Your example can encourage them to express their appreciation as well.
- Give any compliments that are sincere and that you feel comfortable sharing (for example, "I really like the way everyone participates in the discussion").
- Give the leader specific feedback. What did you appreciate about the way he or she led the group meeting? Give the feedback as soon as possible after the meeting, but certainly by the end of the next day. If you wait too long, most leaders will naturally assume the worst.

Be Informed

Group visits are most effective when coaches come fully informed regarding the small group and its members. Before planning a group visit, invest time in your coaching conversations, getting to know not just the leader but also the group.

Here are some key things to consider, items you may want to ask the leader about in a one-on-one conversation as you plan your first group visit.

- What is the nature and purpose of the group?
- How long has the group been together? How did it start?
- What curriculum is the group using? Is the topic for that night sensitive enough in nature that it would be better for you to visit another time?
- Who are the group members?
- When would the leader like you to arrive?
- Does the leader have any concerns about this meeting?
- What role should you play in the meeting? Observer? Participant? (The focus here is on what would make the group and the leader most comfortable.)

Preparation for the Group Visit
Go with a Plan in Mind

As you plan your visit, think through your role and how you can best serve this particular leader and group. Commit the time to prayer, asking God to use you to help the leader and the members grow in their relationship with Christ.

Because you are a guest in the group, the members may change their relating patterns—sharing more or less because of their nervousness. Coaches should plan regular visits to groups so that members become comfortable with their presence. A good rule of thumb is two to three visits per calendar or ministry year.

Meet with the Leader

Several weeks prior to your group visit, meet with the leader and the apprentice. This may be part of a regular coaching conversation or a separate meeting for the sole purpose of planning your visit. When you meet, allow time to do the following:

- Explain to the leader the purpose of the visit.
- Select the best day and time for your visit. Certain types of groups or group studies may require more planning to select an appropriate night for a visit.
- Answer any questions the leader may have about your visit.
- Get the leader's perception of the current status of the group. Include any concerns, reasons to celebrate, or problems.
- Pray with the leader about his group and your visit.
- Remind the leader to inform the members that you will be visiting.

Set Goals

Goals will help you clarify your role during the visit and choose which action to take with the leader and apprentice. Ask yourself these questions regarding your group visit:

- Why am I visiting this group?
- What do I hope to achieve by this visit?

Here are some possible answers to those questions.

For Myself

I hope to get to know the leader and group members better.

I hope to gain an understanding of how the leader relates to the group.

I want to explore how the leader is developing the gift of each group member.

I want to explore how the leader is developing the apprentice.

I want to look for potential leaders who may become apprentices.

I wish to understand the nature of the relationships in the group.

I wish to evaluate the members' level of commitment to this group.

I want to develop the skills of my apprentice coach.

For the Leader

I want to encourage and support this leader.

The leader needs help in assessing a particular situation.

There is an issue or problem that the leader needs help solving.

I want to affirm to group members this leader's commitment (or other qualities).

I want to assist the leader and the group in launching new groups (multiplying).

I would like to help the leader clarify the church's vision for small groups.

I want to challenge the leader and the group to be open to new members.

For the Group Members

I will help the members understand that they have a coach and staff supporting them.

I will answer questions that members might have about the church.

I will answer members' questions about the small group ministry.

I will encourage members in their commitment to attending a small group.

I will affirm members' desire to grow in their relationship with Christ.

Plan the Specifics

Use the planning guide on pages 137–39 to think through the details and goals for your visit. Fill in the top part of the guide with pertinent facts about your visit. This will also serve as a quick reference during the visit. When the visit is over, take a few minutes to compose your thoughts about what you experienced in your time with the group. *Do not* write your thoughts down while in the group meeting. That will definitely not make the group comfortable with your next visit!

PLANNING A GROUP VISIT

Leader's name: _____

Group visit: _____

Meeting time: _____

Time to arrive: _____

Lesson/Topic:

My role in meeting:

On which aspect of coaching does this group visit need to be more focused?

Leadership Skills

Were the objectives of the meeting accomplished?

Did the needs of the group members appear to be served by the meeting? By the leader?

Did the leader involve everyone?

Gift Development

How is the leader developing the gifts of the group members?

How is the leader developing the apprentice leader?

Group Dynamics

How did the group discussion flow?

How well do relationships in the group appear to be growing?

Did there seem to be any unresolved conflict?

Care

How are needs being met in the group?

Do members feel cared for? Celebrated?

How can I pray for this group?

Follow-Up Items

What issues surfaced that I would like to follow up on with this leader and/or group? (This includes items of concern as well as items to celebrate.)

Reflect for a few minutes on your visit with this group. As a coach, how did you support and serve the leader during the visit? What skills would you like to improve so that your group visits are more helpful?

Making the Group Visit

Arrive Early

Plan to meet with the leader and apprentice before the meeting.

- Ask them how they are doing personally.
- Ask them again about the group. Are there any concerns about the meeting?
- Confirm the role they would like you to play in the meeting.
- Discuss the agenda and the leader's plan for the meeting.
- Pray together for them, for the people in the group, and for the meeting.

- Assure them you are there to support them.
- Greet the group members as they arrive.

Observe the Meeting

Ask the leader to introduce you to the group members and remind the group why you are there. Participate at the level that you have agreed upon with the leader. Make sure your participation doesn't limit or inhibit the participation of the members. Remember, the goal of the visit is to observe the group in action. Pay close attention to how the leader and the apprentice interact with the group.

Here are some questions you may wish to include when making your observations after the meeting.

- Was the setting conducive to a good meeting?
- Did the meeting start and end on time?
- Did the leader stay on the subject?
- Was the leader in control but not overbearing?
- Were the questions effective?
- Did the leader listen to the responses?
- How well did the group members relate to each other?
- What is the relationship between the leader and the members?
- Did any member seem to dominate the discussion?
- Is multiplication (birthing) a part of the group's strategy?
- Is the group open to new people? When was the newest member added?
- Was the prayer time meaningful? Who participated?
- How was God at work in this meeting?

Be careful about taking notes during the meeting. It may appear that you are being critical of the group in general or of a specific comment made by a group member. It's best to block out some time soon after the meeting to record your observations in private.

Also, be prepared to leave during part of the meeting if the group needs to share some confidential thoughts or prayer requests. Step out of the room or simply leave early, thanking the group for the opportunity to connect with them.

After the Visit

If possible, prior to leaving the meeting, give some immediate feedback to the leader and apprentice. Share a couple of specific, encouraging thoughts. Ask questions to clarify any part of the meeting that was unclear or confusing to you.

As soon as possible after the visit, schedule another time to meet with the leader and apprentice. Review in detail your thoughts and observations, remembering to be encouraging about the things they did well.

Don't simply point out areas of their leadership that need work; be prepared to offer concrete suggestions for improvement. Give several ideas to choose from, so they can decide which would work best in their group. Be a resource for your leaders.

If a problem surfaced during your visit, be certain to follow up with the leader as often as needed, even if it's several times each week. Work with the leader to bring resolution to the problem.

After the visit, evaluate your own effectiveness as a coach. Look over the comments you wrote down and see if there is anything you could have done differently. If your apprentice coach was with you, discuss the visit together.

Keep a record of your visit to review before the next time you sit in on this group. Use the record as a tool for planning your next visit.

Special Situations

The main purpose of a group visit is to support and encourage the well-being of the leader and the group. If a group visit is done well, everyone should feel encouraged. That bears repeating, because there are special situations in which visiting a group may be counterproductive. It may work *against* the well-being of the group.

In many support and recovery groups, the level of sharing is very deep and requires a significant amount of time to develop. Introducing a stranger into the group—even an "organizationally sanctioned" coach—can break trust in the group for an evening or longer. Depending on the type of group or the individuals in that group, a coach's visit might be enough cause for some people to end their involvement permanently.

That certainly does not fit into the category of helping the well-being of the group—and for that reason, we would not encourage a group visit. Yet we can't write a blanket statement about support and recovery groups, because there are some that would and do welcome a coach's visit.

Truth is, we can't write a blanket statement about any type of group (except for that one). There may be seasons in any group when a coach's visit is not advisable. Sensitive issues are being dealt with in a God-honoring way. It's family business. Mature believers are behaving maturely —and it's a beautiful thing to see when it happens. Sin is being confessed. Problems are being dealt with. Hard truth is being spoken. The group is functioning well, and the coach isn't needed. That's really a good thing.

In those times, the coach will simply reach for other tools—coaching conversations, leadership gatherings—to build into the leader, and trust that the leader will communicate what he or she needs.

Each coach will need to work out which tools will best support, encourage, and help the leader and group *at that particular time*. Every new member added to the group, each month that passes, brings a new texture and new complexity to the group. The needs of the leader can change from one meeting to the next. Crises happen. Groups are messy. *People* are messy. So stay flexible, adaptable. Keep that toolbox handy.

Chapter 4

THE COACH'S LIFE

While the expectations placed on a coach vary from church to church, one fact remains constant: the life of a coach can be as difficult as it is rewarding. Building and sustaining relationships, dealing with crises and challenges, and maintaining clear communication are all tasks demanding chunks of precious time and energy. Most coaches are highly committed volunteers who work in the marketplace or home over fifty hours each week. So how can a coach balance the demands of work and ministry and still have time and energy for his or her family? A hobby? A life? The following guidelines can help coaches

> Your life comes before your ministry!

balance life and ministry. We want to focus on *you* in this chapter. As you will see, it is biblical to focus on your own spiritual growth and leadership capacity, especially as you desire to guide others.

PURSUE CHRISTLIKENESS

The best way coaches can motivate their leaders to live a God-honoring, Christ-centered life is to model that life for them. Without pride or arrogance, simply live the kind of life that God calls us to live, "in such a way that no one will be hindered from finding the Lord by the way we act, and so no one can find fault with our ministry" (2 Cor. 6:3 NLT).

Jesus taught that when modeling is working as it should, the disciple will ultimately become like his teacher (Luke 6:40). Leadership studies have shown this to be true. They confirm that in about thirty-six months, the people you lead will very closely reflect who you are. A loving teacher will produce loving disciples. A joyful teacher typically has disciples who are filled with joy.

The sobering aspect of this principle is that it works whether the values and practices the teacher models are good or bad. Therefore it's critical that you model the right pattern of living for your leaders.

On the surface, modeling can feel haughty or arrogant. Who am I to say that people should follow my example of Christian living?

On a number of occasions, Paul asked—even commanded—others to follow his example. Listen to Paul's coaching to three different churches.

- "I urge you to imitate me.... Follow my example, as I follow the example of Christ" (1 Cor. 4:16; 11:1).
- "Join together in following my example" (Phil. 3:17).
- "You yourselves know how you ought to follow our example" (2 Thess. 3:7).

Paul invested his life in Timothy and Titus, two young men he coached in ministry. He encouraged them to follow his lead and model the Christian life for people in their care (1 Tim. 4:12; Titus 2:7).

Yet if you scan the book of Acts, you will quickly see that Paul was no angel. He had his flaws and shortcomings. He was human, just like us. So how did Paul, and how can we, resolve the tension between the reality of our spiritual condition and the notion of calling others to follow our example?

By being real—by sharing what God is doing in our lives right now. The practice of modeling is not about being perfect. Even as Paul was encouraging the Christians at Philippi to follow his example, he confessed his weaknesses to them. "I'm not saying that I have this all together, that I have it made. But I am well on my way, reaching out for Christ, who has so wondrously reached out for me. Friends, don't get me wrong: By no means do I count myself an expert in all of this, but I've got my eye on the goal" (Phil. 3:12–13 MSG).

This is where good coaching begins. Authentically modeling the life to which God calls us.

Coaches often downplay the effect that their life and example can have on small group leaders. You are an example to the leaders you coach. What you do and how you live your life has a powerful impact. That's why Paul said to Timothy, "Set an example for the believers in speech, in conduct, in love, in faith and in purity" (1 Tim. 4:12). Paul knew that the principles of Christian living are not only taught; they are caught. Knowledge and skill combined with the example of your own life has a transforming effect on your leaders.

BUILDING SUSTAINABILITY: MANAGING LIFE AT WARP SPEED

Test pilot Chuck Yeager's website records a time line of his team's work to break the sound barrier—to be the first to fly planes at more than seven hundred miles per hour, when forty years earlier no one had ever flown! "Chuck Yeager ... demonstrated an unrivaled ability to quickly ferret out and understand an airplane's flaws. Flying constantly at the edge of the envelope ... and then beyond, at a time when accidents were far more common than they are today, Yeager repeatedly demonstrated an uncanny ability to coolly think his way through potentially catastrophic situations, take appropriate action, and bring his ship back."

At one point while testing a plane, Yeager lost control and began spinning on all three axes. He plunged over fifty thousand feet, but he managed to regain control at the twenty-five-thousand-foot level, finally landing the craft safely.

Ever feel like you're flying at the edge of the envelope? Going way too fast? Hurling along at the pace of life, trying to execute a life plan that's full of flaws?

Years of ministry experience has taught us that when our personal life spins out of control, it's for one of two main reasons:

- *Intense pressure.* You know that feeling. There's always more to do than there is time to do it. Longing for the day to have a few more hours or for the week to have one more day. Riding on that edge between under control and out of control.
- *Intoxicating joy.* When things are going well, the joy is incredible! We could do without sleep, food, and vacation days forever ... it feels great! Often, success is intoxicating, and we can't tell when we've had enough.

That's at your job or wherever you invest a large amount of work time, paid or unpaid. Tensions in the workplace are always present, but some seasons heighten them. It seems more people are working more hours with fewer staff and tighter margins. It's true in business, in education, in the home, and in the church. Work pressures keep increasing, and life gets more demanding.

Some of us juggle multiple worlds as single parents or hold more than one job. On top of this, we volunteer in the church. People are more bivocational (in terms of work and volunteerism) than ever.

As a result, a sustainable and reasonable pace of life remains elusive.

So how do we live a sustainable life? How do we manage life at warp speed? Here are three key areas to watch in life, and three key practices that will help you. Like you, we're not perfect. But we are intentional—because if you don't get ahead of the pressure, it will overwhelm you.

Monitor Your Gauges

One of the things you discovered when you learned to drive: watch the gauges on the dash. You can't see or smell or sense a problem in your car as quickly as these gauges can. They'll tell you, if you pay attention.

Spiritual

- How's your personal time with God? Are you feeding yourself regularly from the Word? Or is the only time you open the Bible to prep for coaching leaders or teaching a class?
- How is your heart in worship? Do you find yourself avoiding worship and scheduling meetings with church leaders instead?
- How is your heart toward God?
- How is this gauge? Is the needle moving toward full or empty?

Look at the following gauge and draw an arrow to mark your spiritual capacity at this point in life. Full? Empty? Halfway?

Emotional

- Do your relationships with your spouse, fellow workers, or close friends create or drain energy?
- Are your nerves raw? Is anger or sadness or some other strong emotion frequently near the surface?
- After a conversation or a meeting, do you often find yourself questioning your strong emotional reaction? What was *that* about?
- Not feeling anything these days?

Emotional

Physical

- Are you tired all the time? Maybe it's the new baby, the special needs child, the teenager, or the aging parents. Maybe it's the pressure of balancing life and job and ministry.
- Do you talk about sleep like a starving person talks about food?
- Are you overweight or out of shape? Not caring for yourself physically?
- Are you getting any exercise and replenishing yourself?

Physical

———

Look at all three gauges. How are you doing? Full? Nearly empty? Running on empty?

Do you have the physical, emotional, and spiritual energy to build into your leaders and lead your ministry? Do you have something to give? Anything?

These gauges can drift low—and we can be caught off guard. Be diligent to keep watching all three lest you wind up focused on the wrong gauge!

Be realistic—how is your capacity to lead and serve and live?

Three Keys to Sustainability

1. Set Boundaries

Relationship Boundaries

Be careful to choose two-way, or reciprocal, relationships, not just those in which you are the primary giver and others simply take from you. That will be draining over time.

Schedule Boundaries

Don't always be available. When on vacation, try to avoid cell phone messages, work emails, and unnecessary technology. Try a technology fast. Block time away from interruptions.

- Keep family as a priority. Show your spouse and kids they matter.
- Don't answer phones during a meal.
- Take entire days off away from work and ministry. God's pattern for Sabbath rest is essential.

Ministry Boundaries

Maintain healthy boundaries with the church.

- Watch what you say yes to!
- Beware of the next "great ministry opportunity" that someone offers —there are thousands of great ministry opportunities, and you can't pursue them all.
- If a supervisor asks you to add to your ministry load, try saying, "I can do that, but which of these other priorities would you like me to drop in order to make that happen?"
- Make sure others understand your boundaries!

2. Create Margin

"Margin is the amount allowed beyond what is needed. It is something held in reserve for contingencies or unanticipated situations. Margin is the gap between rest & exhaustion, the space between breathing freely and suffocating. It is the leeway we once had between ourselves and our limits" (Richard Swenson, *Margins*).

Some of us would fill every waking moment with planned activity, leaving no space for spontaneity or emergencies. We are too accustomed to leaving no room for the important things!

Then, when the inevitable happens—death, sickness, or even fun opportunities—we have no margin, no room to add these things to an exhausting schedule without a major reconstruction of our lives.

Create margin in your personal life and in your work life. Give priority to God, your spouse, your children, your work, and then your ministry. And leave room for the unexpected or unanticipated.

Scan your monthly and weekly calendar every Monday.

Or try using the stress calendar (see p. 149) or a similar tool.

How much margin do you really have? Let's continue working for a few pages and see if we can't help you find some hours. Hang in there—relief lies just ahead!

CREATE MARGIN USING A STRESS CALENDAR

1. There are twenty-one boxes in the following table, three for each day of the week. The times are listed to give you a rough idea of the hours in each block.
2. Place an *X* in each box where you have an obligation, even if it's only for an hour. An obligation is something you must be present for, not something you choose to participate in. For example, if you have a night school class that meets for one hour on Tuesdays at 7:00 p.m., place an *X* across the *entire* block of Tuesday evening. After all, you have to drive to the class, expend energy, and drive home. Even for short meetings and obligations, you use up emotional and physical energy.
3. After you have marked your boxes, rate yourself on the scale following the table.

	Mon.	Tues.	Wed.	Thurs.	Fri.	Sat.	Sun.
Morning 7:00–12:00							
Afternoon 1:00–5:00							
Evening 6:00–10:00							

Make sure you include anything that is a "have to," including travel time, preparation time, and recovery time. Sometimes the smallest commitments take the most energy from us. Anything that demands time and energy must be a factor in stress management!

Rating Yourself
19 – 21 boxes filled = headed for burnout
17 – 18 boxes filled = very busy, some margin but potentially stress-filled
14 – 16 boxes filled = lots of margin and room for choices
10 – 13 boxes filled = welcome to retirement
  0 – 9 boxes filled = get a life!

3. Replenish Your Reserves

When you see that your gauges are moving toward empty in one or more areas, you must take steps to remedy the situation and create a new way of life. Refueling or replenishing your reserves allows you to be ready for the energy-draining demands of life and ministry. Here are some suggestions for each area—spiritually, emotionally, and physically.

Spiritually

Those of us in people-intensive work environments need the practice of solitude: time away and space for reflection, rest, hearing God's voice, and gaining back the energy we have lost in ministry activities.

- Jesus withdrew to deserted places for prayer (Luke 4:42; 5:16).
- Before big decisions and ministry challenges, he was alone in prayer (Luke 6:12; 9:18).

Emotionally

Make time to fill up your empty emotional tank with a hobby, a vacation, or occasionally a time of just hanging out with your family and friends (with no agenda).

- What is it that fills you up?
- What activities or environments provide joy and fun?
- What kind of space allows you to clear your brain of all the troubles and issues and struggles?
- When was the last time you did those things that bring you great pleasure, freedom, and joy, alone or with others you love?

Greg likes woodworking; Bill plays guitar. We both enjoy a good ball game or a meal with close friends and family, and we both enjoy reading.

Whatever it is, focus on the things that put fuel in *your* tank—things that give you energy for life and ministry. Avoid the "ought tos" and the "have tos" and invest in some "want tos" and "love tos."

Physically

Care for yourself. We all learn the hard way that we need exercise. Maybe you get some blood work done at the doctor's office, or you feel sluggish, or you just look in the mirror and realize, "This is not good—something needs to change!"

A guilt-driven conscience will shout you down, saying that your work and ministry will suffer if you step away from it to exercise. You will rationalize that time spent for fitness is lost time for productivity. After all, you can always catch up later and start eating right after the next big holiday, birthday, or office party.

You are telling yourself a lie.

Physical exercise and work release endorphins, stimulate the heart and other muscles, improve mental acuity, increase current and long-term energy levels, and simply make you look, work, and feel better.

———

So how are your gauges, and what are you doing about it?

Here's the big question: Is my pace sustainable—can I continue this pace for the long term with the current way I'm doing life and ministry?

Dallas Willard remarked, "It is the responsibility of every Christian to carve out a satisfying life under the rule of God—so that sin won't look so good."

Our hope and prayer for you is that you will do that! You will take the steps to bring rhythm and harmony to your life. Live the abundant life Jesus promised!

REFLECTION

It can be overwhelming to try to reorient every aspect of your life in the next few moments. And it can be a daunting task to lay out a detailed five-year plan that you will follow with discipline and fervor. Instead start small and specific. Build habits and practices one at a time, then add more along the way.

What one thing can you begin to do (or stop doing), or what targeted change can you make, that will help you in the next thirty days? Perhaps starting one new spiritual practice, returning to a fun hobby you've neglected, putting boundaries around a relationship, or remaking your calendar. Look at the three areas below and list something in each area. Then choose one area to start with. Later you can add the others, perhaps over the next sixty to ninety days.

Small changes can produce profound results.

Spiritual:

Emotional:

Physical:

As we look closely at the ministry of Jesus, we see that his pace was never hurried or hectic. He maintained a balance between his larger, public ministry and time spent in more personal settings. It was not uncommon for Jesus to spend several days teaching, healing, and being with the masses. But then he withdrew and refueled (Matt. 14:13; Mark 1:35; 6:32; Luke 4:42).

Jesus maintained a healthy rhythm in the midst of huge demands and challenges in his life and ministry. *Do not* strive for perfect balance. "I will spend two hours in prayer, two hours serving others, and two hours playing golf." If that is balance, then life will throw you off balance almost every day.

Building rhythm, on the other hand, recognizes that life demands times of intensity (extra work hours, a family crisis, a brief illness or injury, and so on). But then, after that intense period is over, a person compensates for what was neglected and adds time for rest, reflection, fun, and joy.

Plan Your Activities

Knowing what to do and having a plan are not the same thing. You need a plan.

In a relational ministry such as coaching, the work is never truly completed. New issues that need your attention will regularly surface. New problems will arise and will need to be resolved. Leaders will constantly need fresh vision and skills. Your work will resemble a marathon more closely than a sprint. And good marathoners know that staying in the race means establishing a sustainable pace. Here are some strategies to help you set the right pace.

Take a look at your personal calendar (see sample on p. 155), and look again at your stress calendar from the exercise above. Begin by setting aside time each week, or at least each month, for the following:

- Personal time with God
- Work obligations
- Time with family and friends
- Attending church services

Now, assuming there is any time left in your schedule, determine the best time for you to invest in your leaders. As a starting point, choose one coaching activity a week. For example, in a typical four-to-six-week period, most coaches can be expected to do the following:

- Visit one small group meeting
- Have a one-on-one meeting with a group leader

- Conduct a leadership gathering for their group leaders
- Meet with a ministry leader or staff member
- Participate in a leadership gathering with other coaches
- Maintain regular contact with each leader through phone and email

Mark these items on your calendar as well.

Now take a look at the calendar overall. Is the pace sustainable? Are you filling in too many boxes and heading toward burnout? Let's put the margin concept into action now that you know your priorities and your boundaries (changes you might need to make after reviewing the results from the stress calendar).

To help avoid burnout, schedule two more items on your calendar: margin and replenishment. Create open, unplanned spaces on your calendar —even if you have to write them in as "margin." Then set aside times to replenish yourself with a hobby, vacation, recreation, exercise, or rest. Block off these times on your calendar and guard them carefully. They are keys to your health and your ability to thrive long-term in the coaching role.

Revisiting the Stress Calendar

Now that you have reflected on changes you need to make, test them against your revised stress calendar. Will things be different? Can you maintain the pace? Try to design the best rhythm you can, knowing that in any given month life will ebb and flow.

REVISED STRESS CALENDAR							
	Mon.	Tues.	Wed.	Thurs.	Fri.	Sat.	Sun.
Morning 7:00–12:00							
Afternoon 1:00–5:00							
Evening 6:00–10:00							

Maximize Your Time

You have a limited amount of time to invest in coaching your leaders. For that reason, it's important to concentrate on the goals and activities that advance your ministry to them. In some seasons, your leaders will be better served if you concentrate on one aspect of the coaching role, like one-on-one meetings. That extra time in individual meetings may mean that you lessen the frequency of leadership gatherings or group visits. Remember, the goal is not to hold meetings! It's to develop and nurture your leaders.

To make the most of your time, you may also want to double up on meetings or appointments. Suppose you are going to visit a group on Tuesday night. Could you save another night out by meeting with another leader before or after the visit?

Use the personal calendar (p. 155) as an exercise, a practice calendar if you will, to schedule your week, seeking to avoid stress and create margin. Using the big-picture ideas and commitments from the stress calendar, create a more specific personal calendar with actual time slots. It may not be perfect, but the exercise will force you to test reality against your desires and discern where adjustments are needed.

Know When to Step Down

Sometimes life is just too crazy or demands are too overwhelming for you to continue in your role, at least for a season. An honest conversation with a church staff member is needed to process this and gain wisdom.

To be a coach is to serve in a high-impact role in the church. The sky is the limit on making a difference, but the pressures and demands can be intense as well. Problems rarely surface at a convenient time, people can be messy, conflict resolution is seldom neat and tidy, and the list goes on and on.

Even when coaches do their best to establish and maintain a healthy rhythm, things change. Life circumstances can impact your coaching. Personal illness or struggles, family challenges such as aging parents or special needs in your children, a change or loss of employment—all have an impact on your capacity for ministry.

Because of the close relationship that often develops between coaches and their leaders, making the decision to step down can be very difficult. The close ties can cloud your judgment, and knowing when to quit can be tough.

Some coaches want to wave the white flag too soon. When their first small group experiences conflict or trouble, or when a leader doesn't respond immediately to their leadership, they take these difficulties as an indicator that they have failed and should step down.

There are others who more closely resemble first-century martyrs. In spite of personal struggle and loss, they refuse to quit. They are determined to persevere; to quit would be viewed as failure. The truth is, these coaches

PERSONAL CALENDAR

Time	Mon.	Tues.	Wed.	Thurs.	Fri.	Sat.	Sun.
8:00 a.m.							
10:00 a.m.							
Noon							
2:00 p.m.							
4:00 p.m.							
6:00 p.m.							
8:00 p.m.							
10:00 p.m.							

often hang on too long, to the detriment of their leaders and of their own soul.

So how do you know when the load is too heavy? How do you know when you need to take a break from coaching? Here are some questions to help you think through this tough issue. Do a quick checkup and put a check mark beside the statements that are true for you.

- ☐ It has been more than three weeks since I've had any contact with my leaders.
- ☐ When I think about how I'm doing as a coach, I feel shame or guilt.
- ☐ I continually feel that ministry demands are overwhelming.
- ☐ I feel resentment when the church staff or group leaders make demands of me.
- ☐ I find myself having strong reactions to ministry difficulties.
- ☐ I struggle to fully engage my heart in worship.
- ☐ My desire to practice spiritual disciplines is decreasing.

☐ I constantly feel hurried, wishing for one more hour or day to get things done.

☐ Intense emotions, anger, or sadness seem to be always near the surface.

While this list is not exhaustive, checking off more than two items ought to cause you some concern. Either the ministry demands are too great (whether imposed by yourself or others) or your capacity has diminished. Did you check four or more? You're in the danger zone.

A conversation with a staff member or senior coach would be a good start to figuring out why you feel this pressure and what can be done to resolve it. You may be expecting too much of yourself. You may have misunderstood the church's expectations of coaches. Perhaps you've signed up to volunteer in other ministries in the church, and the combined expectations are overwhelming. Or you may be in a season of life in which the demands of coaching are too much for you.

Whatever the reason, do yourself and your leaders a favor. Sit down with a staff member or ministry leader and talk through this. Spend time alone with God in prayer, seeking his heart for you. Seek out godly counsel to help determine if you should take a break from coaching.

THREE ESSENTIAL PERSONAL SPIRITUAL PRACTICES

There are many personal spiritual disciplines, or practices, that help keep you connected to God and engaged in your faith. (See appendix 1 for a full list.) You shouldn't try to start them all at once if this is a new area for you. However, there are three personal/spiritual practices that everyone should incorporate regularly into life. Combined with corporate practices (worship, participation in the Lord's Supper, and so on), which should be shared with your local church community, these three personal practices will keep you grounded.

PRACTICE 1: Study

Reading the Bible regularly is food for the hungry soul, knowledge for the searching mind, and encouragement for the fainting heart. I have learned various ways of reading and studying the Bible over the years, especially from other leaders and teachers in the church, both current and through the ages.

Guidelines for Bible Reading

Study the Bible for yourself, but not *just by yourself.* Yes, learn to study the Bible. Take online courses; wrestle with the text; do your own work. Spend time alone digging into the Word of God. But don't stop there! Talk with others, use commentaries and reference guides. Listen to teachers on the sections or topics you are studying. Your understanding of the text is important, but it could be prejudiced, narrow, or even wrong. Others in the body of Christ, especially those with teaching and scholarship gifts, can help you understand what you are reading.

Never engage the text without encountering the Author. Too many people fall in love with the Bible and rarely find themselves in deep fellowship with the primary writer—God! When you read, expect to meet God. Expect to feel his presence and to hear his voice and to sense his life in you. Don't just let your mind be captured by the truth; let your heart be captivated by Jesus.

Read the Bible for transformation, not just information. Read the Bible asking these questions: How shall I now live? What difference does knowing this make? Then pray: Holy Spirit, please place your finger on areas of life where I need to change and grow and turn toward God.

Three Approaches to Reading the Bible

These methods can be used as a group or alone. In this section, let's focus on your own Bible reading.

1. Read and Reflect

There are four movements in this approach.

1. *Prepare your heart.* Sit quietly or listen to worship music or read a devotional thought to open your heart to God. If you need coffee, get it. If you need a quiet place, find it. Take time to be quiet before God, allowing the clutter and noise to subside in your head.
2. *Listen to the Word.* Read the text several times. Read it slowly, repeatedly, and with a heart that seeks to meet God.
3. *Meditate.* Take words, phrases, or truths that emerge from the text and chew on them. Think about them. Ponder their significance. Repeat them in your head or out loud. Consider memorizing some of it. Take time to reflect on the significance of these words. What is God saying to you, to his church, to our world?

4. *Respond.* Consider the action you must take. Sometimes it is simply to sit and enjoy God and his truth. Sometimes there is something to obey or someone you might need to meet with.

The focus in this method is to simply commune with God and enjoy his presence. Trust the Word and the Spirit to speak.

2. Engage and Examine

In this approach, read the text and engage with the deep and challenging phrases or truths in the passage. Here you will not simply meditate on it or think about it—you will study the passage more rigorously.

- *Ask questions of the text.* What is it saying? What words are repeated or important? Who is the audience? Who is the author? What is the purpose of the book or section? What truths or promises are listed? What is the context? What is the setting and culture?
- *Determine what it meant and what it means.* What did the author want the original audience to know? In light of their culture and setting and spiritual condition, what was the writer communicating? Try to discern what truths, principles, or commands also apply to our lives and culture today. You will likely need a study Bible, a Bible dictionary, a commentary on that book of the Bible, and other written or online resources. Ask your church leaders what they recommend for Bible study tools and resources.
- *Search the Scriptures for similar texts or themes or ideas.* Use the concordance at the back of the Bible, or the cross-references in the margins. Start with passages in the same book of the Bible, then from the same author, then go to other references. Where else did the writers of Scripture talk about this truth, place, idea, or character?
- *Summarize the learning or wrestle with the tension, the unknown.* Given the time you have, pause and try to summarize what you have learned from your study. Write down some conclusions or questions that you still have. How would you teach what you have learned to a ten-year-old? That is a good test.

3. Observe and Obey

The focus on this approach is heavily on the "so what?" How shall we now *live*?

- Read the text and observe what the main teachings and themes are. Look for specific commands and guidelines for a life of faithfulness.

- Now ask, "God, how can I obey you here? What action must I take to bring my life in line with your truth?"

Be Aware That Each Approach Has Challenges

Remember, no approach is flawless or will do full justice to all the richness of the Bible. You can spend weeks on a given passage and only scratch the surface. That is the beauty and wonder of the Bible. Though very simple and clear, enough for even a child to understand, it also holds deep truths and mysteries that take years to fully grasp, experience, and practice. The well never runs dry.

Here are some cautions for each method.

Read and reflect. You might be tempted to ignore challenging passages or avoid rigor required in the text, shying away from studying it later.

Engage and examine. This can become an intellectual exercise if learning content and gathering information become the focus.

Observe and obey. You might move too quickly to application without reflection, meeting the Author, sitting with the truth you are reading.

Of course, you could take a text and use all three approaches in a given week. Generally, the passage of the Bible and your own growth needs will help you discern which approach is best for any given reading exercise. If you have only a few minutes, approach 1 or approach 3 might be best. If you are preparing for a lesson, approach 2 would be good, assuming you have at least an hour.

PRACTICE 2: Prayer

Effective coaches have vital prayer lives. Here are some guidelines to help you become a more effective coach and person of prayer. We've found them to be useful and powerful principles.

First we'll give you an outline for praying, then some principles for prayer from Romans 8, and then some prerequisites for answered prayer.

An Outline for Prayer—ACTS

Adoration (Ps. 100)

1. Choose one of God's attributes; praise him for his character.
2. Paraphrase a psalm.
3. Pray back a psalm.

Confession (1 John 1:9). Take an inventory of yesterday. Is there anything there that displeases the Lord? Make a list, ask for and receive God's forgiveness, then destroy the list.

Thanksgiving (Luke 17:11–19; 1 Thess. 5:16–18). List your blessings, using the following categories:

1. Spiritual
2. Relational
3. Material
4. Physical

Supplication (Phil. 4:6–7; 1 John 5:14–15). Categorize your needs under the following headings:

1. Major concerns
2. Relational
3. Physical or material
4. Spiritual
5. Character

Listen quietly—wait for the Spirit to lead and guide. (For more on this, see Bill Hybels's book *Too Busy Not to Pray.*)

Four Principles of Prayer: Romans 8:26–29

Romans 8:26–29 gives us some insights into prayer. As you read the passage and meditate on it, you will find some of the principles listed below. God certainly answers prayer, but not always in the way we expect. This information will help you understand how God responds to prayer.

1. The Holy Spirit helps us to know what and how to pray (v. 26).
2. The Holy Spirit intercedes on our behalf (v. 26).
3. God hears our hearts more than the words in prayer (v. 27).
4. Prayer is always answered (vv. 28–29), though not always according to our agenda. There are four possible responses to our prayers.

No. Your request is not in God's will (2 Sam. 12:15–16, 22–23; Matt. 26:36–39).

Slow. Your request is not in God's will at this time (Gen. 15:2–6; 21:2; John 11:3, 6, 14–15, 17, 43–44).

Grow. Your motives are wrong (Num. 14:26–45; James 4:3).

Go. Your request, timing, and spiritual condition are okay. Yes! (1 Kings 18:36–39; [cf. James 5:17–18]; Acts 12:5–7, 12–17).

Prerequisites for Answered Prayer

Though it is clear from Scripture that God always answers our prayers in some manner (as we mentioned above), there are also some guidelines for effective praying. Certain practices or attitudes can hinder your prayers, and in such cases God will not respond to them. The passages below help us understand that we must be in a right relationship with God and with others in order for God to hear our prayers.

> Harboring unconfessed sin will put a barrier between you and God (Ps. 66:18).
>
> God hears the prayers of people who obey his commands (1 John 3:22–23).
>
> God will not hear the prayers of people who have wrong or selfish motives (James 4:3).
>
> We are instructed to pray according to God's will, not according to ours (1 John 5:14–15).
>
> When we pray, we are to ask in faith. Unbelief is a barrier to answered prayer (Mark 11:22–24).
>
> An ongoing abiding life in Christ (having regular fellowship with him) will allow your prayers to be heard. However, when fellowship is broken, so is communication with God (John 15:7).
>
> Sometimes we don't have answered prayers because we do not ask. We are to pursue appropriate requests regularly and bring them to God (Luke 11:9).
>
> Praying in the Spirit (that is, under the control of the Holy Spirit) is also a prerequisite. We must also persevere in our praying (Eph. 6:18).
>
> If you do not forgive someone for wrongs that person has done to you, then God will not forgive you. Restored and right relationships are essential for open communication with God (Matt. 6:14–15; Mark 11:25).
>
> We are to pray with thankful hearts. Those of us who come before God without a spirit of thankfulness will find that our prayers are not heard (Phil. 4:6).

Four Guidelines for Prayer
- Pray to God about everything (Phil. 4:6–7).
- Pray consistently (1 Thess. 5:17).
- Pray according to the name of Jesus — that is, according to the will of Jesus (John 16:24).
- Pray with bold confidence (Heb. 4:16).

PRACTICE 3: Community

Coaches need community for the same reasons everyone else does. You need a place to be known and loved, a place for taking faith risks, and a place where you can be challenged to develop spiritually.

If we desire to remain in Christ and grow in him, we need community. Yet finding a small group in which it's safe to be real and vulnerable can be a challenge for coaches. When a coach walks into a group, a certain level of skill and wisdom are assumed by the members and the leader. It can be difficult to take off the coach hat and put on a member hat.

So where and how can coaches find community? Some experience community as they meet with their leaders or fellow coaches in leadership gatherings. Others find a type of community as they meet one-on-one with their leaders. While both of these experiences are good, they will not fully meet a coach's need for community.

Here are two possible solutions.

1. *Join an existing small group.* For many coaches, this is usually a men's or women's group. But it can also be a mixed group. The key is what you find there. Just be sure to establish clear boundaries and expectations with the leader and the group. Be clear that you are attending simply as a member, not as a coach. You are there to participate, not to evaluate or guide.

2. *Form a coaches' community.* Jesus connected more deeply with Peter, James, and John. Paul often had one or two close partners with him, doing ministry and sharing life (Titus, Luke, Timothy, Priscilla, and Aquila). So what about you? You may want to consider forming a small group with other coaches. Be careful that this is really community and not just a business meeting.

A Band of Brothers, a Society of Sisters

Every coach needs a relational support network. Your life in an authentic community will provide the care, the opportunities for personal growth, and the place to simply "be" that you need. When coaches fail to experience such a community—whether by joining an existing small group or forming a coaches' community—they will eventually find their souls withering and their hearts becoming despondent.

Here are some questions to ask about such a group for you, a coach seeking community.

Does the group treat me as a leader in a role or as a person in relationship? (You want the latter.)

Is this a place where I find safety and friendship?

Does the community offer accountability that is not judgmental but rather inspirational, where we come alongside one another to help each other stay the course and work through sin or brokenness?

Can I share frustrations about ministry challenges without fear that others in the group will become discouraged with the church?

Are there one or two others in the group who could be close spiritual friends with whom I share deeply and confess the deeper personal needs and faults I have?

Is there a culture of grace and truth which, over time, will allow me to walk more closely with Christ and others?

Do others in the group understand the specific needs, disappointments, and frustrations that accompany leadership in a spiritual setting?

Working through these questions will help you and potential members of the group create the environment necessary for real community.

Relational integrity stems directly from authentic communal engagement. You are, at some level, the product of your community. Living with others, as Jean Vanier says, reveals our pride and ego, and yet it gives opportunities to be "for" others and share their lives. This practice keeps every coach from thinking too highly of himself or herself and from self-absorption.

REFLECTION

My Personal Community

Take a few moments to think and pray about who might be in your inner circle of friends (perhaps some fellow coaches and leaders), people with whom you can share life and speak the truth in love.

Your life and leadership matter to the church. The words of Paul to Timothy are again appropriate: *"Pay close attention to yourself* and to your teaching"* (1 Tim. 4:16 NASB, emphasis ours).

FINAL THOUGHTS

We cheer you on as you continue to accomplish the ministry of coaching. It's a privilege to work with leaders. We pray that your experience as a coach will be rewarding to you personally and have great impact in the lives of the people you lead.

Keep using this manual as a resource for your growth and as a tool to train and equip other coaches and group leaders.

Let us know if we can serve your church as trainers or speakers. It would be our privilege to help in any way. You can contact us at *www.drbilldonahue.com*.

Remain constant in prayer to God the Father, connected to his community, the church, committed to Jesus Christ, rooted in the Word, and guided by the Spirit!

"Continue in what you have learned and have become convinced of, because you know those from whom you learned it, and how from infancy you have known the Holy Scriptures, which are able to make you wise for salvation through faith in Christ Jesus. All Scripture is God-breathed and is useful for teaching, rebuking, correcting and training in righteousness, so that the servant of God may be thoroughly equipped for every good work" (2 Tim. 3:14–17 NIV 2011).

PERSONAL SPIRITUAL PRACTICES

WHY ARE SPIRITUAL PRACTICES SO IMPORTANT?

Note: If you are using Leading Life-Changing Small Groups *with your group leaders, you will find this material there as well. By having a copy for yourself here, you'll be able to use it for personal growth and can refer to it when having one-on-one meetings or phone calls with leaders.*

The apostle Paul compares the Christian life to running a marathon. We run to win, reaching forward to what lies ahead, always pressing on toward the goal for the prize of the upward call of God in Christ Jesus. The runner, like the Christian, has a goal, a strategy, and a finish line (1 Cor. 9:24–27; Phil. 3:12–14). A race takes stamina, diligence, preparation, and discipline. If we were runners, we would never try to enter a race without proper training. In training, we learn to pursue certain practices that will enable us to endure the race.

In 1 Corinthians 9:24–27 Paul says, "Do you not know that in a race all the runners run, but only one gets the prize? Run in such a way as to get the prize. Everyone who competes in the games goes into strict training. They do it to get a crown that will not last; but we do it to get a crown that will last forever. Therefore I do not run like a man running aimlessly; I do not fight like a man beating the air. No, I beat my body and make it my slave so that after I have preached to others, I myself will not be disqualified for the prize" (NIV 1984).

Spiritual "disciplines," or practices, will help you live the Christian life with authenticity, stamina, and perseverance. You practice these disciplines in preparation for hearing God's voice. They prepare you for the race you were intended to run. Hebrews 5:8 says that Jesus "learned obedience from what he suffered."

The disciplines prepare you to meet God and understand his will, to battle temptation, to engage in loving relationships, to make wise and godly decisions, to love your family, and to be a leader in your area of ministry. There is great joy in being disciplined enough to finish the race. Paul wrote at the end of his life, "I have fought the good fight, I have finished the race, I have kept the faith. Now there is in store for me the crown of righteousness, which the Lord, the righteous Judge, will award to me on that day —and not only to me, but also to all who have longed for his appearing" (2 Tim. 4:7–8). Like Paul, be a leader who finishes the race well.

WHAT ARE THE SPIRITUAL DISCIPLINES?

Dallas Willard, in *The Spirit of the Disciplines*, and Richard Foster, in *Celebration of Discipline*, have compiled a list of spiritual disciplines and practices that they believe Christ modeled. These disciplines are typically organized into two categories: the disciplines of abstinence (or letting go) and the disciplines of engagement.

Disciplines of Letting Go

These practices allow us to relinquish something in order to gain something new. We abstain from busyness in ministry, family life, and work. We stop talking for a while to hear from God. We give up buying another material possession to experience God more fully. First Peter 2:11 warns us to "abstain from sinful desires, which war against your soul." Identify what is keeping you from experiencing greater strength and perspective. Do you talk too much? Are possessions controlling you? Are you too worried about what others think? Choose disciplines that will help you become more dependent on God.

> *Solitude: spending time alone to be with God.* Find a quiet place to be alone with God for a period of time. Use the Bible as a source of companionship with God. Listen to him. Remain alone and still.
>
> *Silence: removing noisy distractions to hear from God.* Find a quiet place away from noise to hear from God. Write your thoughts and impressions as God directs your heart. Silence can occur even in the midst of noise and distraction. But you must focus your attention on your soul. This could mean talking less or talking only when necessary. And it could mean turning off the radio and the TV.
>
> *Fasting: skipping a meal (or meals) to find greater nourishment from God.* Choose a period of time to go without food. Drink water and, if necessary, take vitamin supplements. Feel the pain of having an empty stomach and depend on God to fill you with his grace.

Frugality: learning to live with less money and still meet basic needs. Before buying something new, choose to go without or pick a less expensive alternative that will serve your basic needs. Live a simple, focused life.

Chastity: choosing to abstain from sexual pleasures for a time (those pleasures that are deemed morally right in the bond of marriage) to find higher fulfillment in God. Decide together as a couple to set aside time to go without sexual pleasures in order to experience a deeper relationship with God in prayer.

Secrecy: serving God without self-promotion, so others are unaware of our service. Give in secret. Serve behind the scenes in a ministry that you are assured few will know about.

Sacrifice: giving overabundantly of our resources to remind us of our dependence on Christ. Choose to give more of your time or finances to God than you normally would.

Disciplines of Engagement

Dallas Willard writes, "The disciplines of abstinence must be counter-balanced and supplemented by disciplines of engagement (activity)." Choosing to participate in activities nurtures our souls and strengthens us for the race ahead.

Study: spending time reading the Scriptures and meditating on their meaning and importance in our lives. Scripture is our source of spiritual strength. Choose a time and a place to feed from it regularly.

Worship: offering praise and adoration to God. His praise should continually be on our lips and in our thoughts. Read psalms, hymns, or spiritual songs, or sing to God daily using a praise CD. Keep praise ever before you as you think of God's activity and presence in your life.

Service: choosing to be a humble servant, as Christ was to his disciples when he washed their feet. Consider opportunities to serve in the church and in the community. Learn to do acts of kindness that otherwise might be overlooked (help someone do yard work, clean a house, buy groceries, run an errand, and so on).

Prayer: talking with God about your relationship with him and about the concerns of others. Prayer involves both talking to God and listening to him. Find time to pray without the distraction of people or things. Combine your prayer time with meditation on the Scriptures in order to focus on Christ.

Community: mutual caring and ministry in the body of Christ. Meet regularly with other Christians to find ways to minister to others. Encourage one another.

Confession: regularly admitting your sins to the Lord and to other trusted individuals. As often as you are aware of sin in your life, confess it to the Lord and to those you may have offended.

Submission: humbling yourself before God and others while seeking accountability in relationships. Find faithful brothers or sisters in Christ who can lovingly hold you accountable for your actions and for your growth in Christ.

As you can see, that is a very large list. It can be overwhelming. These practices are not meant for immediate consumption, like a fast-food dinner on the way to a soccer game. They are exercises for the spiritual life, which is a marathon, not a sprint. As you mature and as you move through the various seasons of life, you will face challenges and opportunities that will drive you toward certain disciplines. You will find yourself learning new practices along the way, especially as you connect with other believers and leaders who are using those exercises for personal growth.

KEY COACHING RESOURCES

Becoming a Coaching Leader by Dan Harkayy, CEO of Building Champions, Inc. (Nashville: Nelson, 2007). This is targeted at executives and the business world but has many great strategies and insights for helping leaders achieve great performance.

Leadership Coaching: The Disciplines, Skills and Heart of a Coach by Tony Stoltzfus (Coach 22 Resources and BookSurge, LLC, *www.BookSurge.com*, 2007). Stoltzfus is one of the best trainers of coaches and has a number of resources and tools for developing leaders through coaching. He has a Christian perspective and value system behind his coaching and works with pastors, church leaders, and marketplace professionals. Go to *www.coach22.com* for a variety of resources from Stoltzfus and other leaders in the field of coaching.

They Call Me Coach by John Wooden (New York: McGraw-Hill, 2003). This inspirational book has much wisdom and insight from someone who knew how to bring out the best in people, something every coach should aspire to do.

Developing the Leaders around You by John Maxwell (Nashville: Nelson, 2003). Maxwell focuses on your personal investment into leaders and how to motivate leaders, equip them, and empower them for effectiveness and success.

COACHING HOT POTATOES

DEALING WITH A CARE CRISIS

Sometimes a need in the group exceeds the group's ability to handle it. Such needs include serious medical issues, sudden death of or severe trauma to a family member, marital breakdown, financial disaster, natural disaster or loss of property, and severe emotional stress or mental illness, to name a few.

Here are some principles to use for helping a group leader meet a crisis or for caring for a leader in crisis.

1. There are no quick fixes to deep problems. This will take time.
2. Help the group and the leader move toward the group member, not away from them. Show you care. Express empathy, not advice. If the person in crisis is one of your leaders, the same applies.
3. Showing compassion means to suffer alongside someone. Get in their world and be with them in their trauma.
4. One person's pain affects others. Be aware of the ripple affect a crisis can have in a group or with other leaders.
5. Sometimes a person or leader must leave the group for a season. But don't let them be without community or friendship. They may not come to meetings, but they are part of the group and church.
6. Pray for the person. Let them know that you care and that you believe God will help them as they face this trauma.
7. Clarify the needs and the way you or the group can help. If necessary, lovingly hold the person accountable to action steps they must take to move toward healing.
8. Process this with the whole group, as a group. This may be awkward, but when there is a severe crisis in a member's life (or in the leader's life), it affects the environment of the group, the focus of meetings,

the care requirements, and so on. The group should *not* be expected to meet needs it can't meet. Set boundaries and discuss how to help the person while continuing to be a group and care for one another.

9. Get outside help from your leadership at the church (pastors and others) who deal with crisis situations. They will help you know what you can do and what is beyond your ability.

10. Emergency or life-threatening issues or abuse must be reported immediately to your pastor or emergency professionals. (Check with your church leaders about the kinds of situations that, if you become aware of them, should be immediately shared with someone in authority. See the section on page 172 titled "When *Not* to Honor Confidentiality.")

NAVIGATING A CONFLICT BETWEEN A LEADER AND OTHERS IN A GROUP

When a leader and one or more group members have conflict, a mediator is often necessary. Since the group leader is an authority figure, the member or members may perceive that they don't stand on equal footing. So they might expect you to side with the leader's point of view or description of the problem.

As much as possible, declare that your role is to facilitate a discussion that promotes conflict resolution. Here are some things to do in that role.

1. Describe your role to the participants. You are there to guide the conflict resolution process, not take sides.

2. Encourage each party to clearly explain the problem or situation as they see it. Tell them to make their comments without making judgments yet.

3. Require each party to fully listen to the other party and *repeat* what the other person said. Ask person A, "What did you hear B saying? Do you understand their point of view?"

4. Do a clarity check: does each party fully understand what the other is saying and feeling? Let them express this to one another.

5. Ask, "What are each of you expecting from the other to bring resolution to this?"

6. Help them move toward agreement, forgiveness, and a commitment to restore the relationship.

7. Communicate the results to the group. Usually the group is aware of the relational discord and would benefit to know that it's resolved.

This resolution is a great example of building community and of the humility of a leader to engage in the process of reconciliation.

8. If possible, meet with the group and commend the leader, the member (or members) involved, and the group for the willingness to face conflict and resolve it together.

WHEN *NOT* TO HONOR CONFIDENTIALITY

Although rare, there are times when physical abuse, injury to a minor, sexual abuse, drug abuse, and illegal activity may be encountered among members (or by members) of a group. Or you may become aware that it is taking place outside the group in the life of a group member or their family.

Do not act simply on hearsay or rumor, but if there is known activity of one of the kinds listed above, it must be reported to authorities. Consult your church leadership immediately if you have any doubts. They will have a list of the types of situations that require a coach or group leader to report the behavior.

Of course, in a medical emergency, call 911 first, and then contact a pastor or supervisor.

MEN AND WOMEN IN COACHING RELATIONSHIPS

There will be times when men and women find themselves in a coaching relationship with one another, regardless of your structure or the theology of your church regarding the leadership roles of men and women. Couples may be mentoring couples, or a team leader may have members of the opposite sex who need some coaching.

Coaches serve under the authority of their local church leadership. Whether it's appropriate for men and women to be involved in a coach-leader relationship will most likely be determined by the elders or the governing body of your church.

Coaches should also be mindful of the context in which they serve, considering the culture of their church and that of the surrounding community. Some cultures would view it as inappropriate for a man and woman to meet together in a coaching relationship. To do so in this cultural context could damage the reputation of those involved or of the church.

If you coach leaders of the opposite sex, the following statement from the New Testament may serve as a helpful guideline. "Do not rebuke an older man harshly, but exhort him as if he were your father. Treat younger men as brothers, older women as mothers, and younger women as sisters, with absolute purity" (1 Tim. 5:1–2).

Three Tests for Relational Purity

It's important to constantly examine the thoughts and attitudes of your heart (Heb. 4:12) in order to maintain relational purity. Asking another coach, a spouse, or a staff member to serve as an accountability partner is also helpful. Regularly share your schedule with them and give them permission to ask questions about anything that appears inappropriate.

Before scheduling or conducting a meeting with a leader of the opposite sex, ask yourself these questions:

1. Is there anything impure about my thoughts or intentions in regard to this person?
2. Would I change my actions or my relating patterns toward this individual if another person were present at the meeting, such as my spouse or a trusted friend?
3. Would I change my behavior or relating patterns with this individual if the content of our conversation were to be shared publicly at our next worship service?

If the answer to any of these questions is yes, you should do one or more of the following:

- Postpone or cancel your meeting with the leader.
- Seek out wise counsel and accountability from a friend, spouse, or staff member.
- Ask your small group point person to find a new coach for this leader.

Meeting Guidelines

1. If you are meeting with a member of the opposite sex, have the meeting in public and make sure others know you are meeting. When possible, include a third party in the meeting. Do not meet alone, behind closed doors, or in a secluded area.
2. Avoid physical contact that may be misunderstood as a romantic or sexual advance. Try to sit where there is a natural boundary between you (such as a table) rather than next to one another.
3. Keep the meeting focused on strategic ministry issues and leadership concerns. If the conversation begins to focus on personal, emotional issues, ask for another meeting time and include another person with you (of the same gender as the person you are coaching).

REMOVING A LEADER

There are times when it's necessary to ask a small group leader to step aside. This may be the result of serious moral issues or impropriety, gross negligence, rebellious attitudes and character flaws, or just prolonged ineffectiveness.

Dealing with this requires many skills, not the least of which is confrontation. Confrontation is simply facing reality, speaking the truth in love, and taking the necessary steps to rectify a situation or the wrongdoing that is taking place.

Here are some guidelines.

1. *Never do this alone.* If the situation is looking serious and you are having concerns about a leader, immediately speak to a pastor or supervisor in your coaching ministry.

2. *Pray through this.* The Holy Spirit will help you think through your motives and your process as you address this difficult issue. Pray for wisdom (James 1:2 – 8).

3. *Speak the truth by making observations, not accusations.* "Here is what I see, feel, hear, and so on" is the language to use (Eph. 4:15, 25).

4. *When you first observe problems that warrant a discussion with a leader, go to the leader directly to resolve them.* Obviously, if there is a major issue involving criminal behavior or abuse or other overt destructive actions, contact your pastor immediately. Otherwise first go to the leader and share your observations about their attitude or performance, what the concerns are, and what you expect of them in order to correct the situation. Keep a written record of the conversation in a confidential, secure file.

5. *Develop a plan of action.* Meet with the leader to address the issue, assuming it can be corrected. Discuss accountability and when the issue needs to be addressed and resolved.

6. *Removal.* Assuming there is no satisfactory resolution, *contact your pastor or supervisor* and begin discussions about the process of removing the leader from an active leadership role. Allow the church leadership to guide this process so that you are protected from any accusations concerning the integrity of your decision. As mentioned above, don't do this alone. Matthew 18:15 – 17 describes how to confront someone and when to bring in others to help in the process.

7. *Speak to the group.* With another church leader, meet with the group to describe in general the process you worked through and the

reasons for removal, *if appropriate*. Consult with church leadership as to what needs to be shared with the group. Be careful here, especially if there is some reason for removal that the group was unaware of. If needed, contact the church's legal counsel.

Here are some thoughts for you and your pastor (or others) to consider when you speak to the group members.

Remind them that leadership includes accountability and that the group needs to be protected from leadership that goes awry.

Discuss the nature of community and the need for groups and leaders to work with integrity.

Speak the whole truth to whom the whole truth is due. Not everyone needs to hear everything about the situation. Choose appropriate talking points and assure the group that the process was biblical and that you are working to correct and restore the leader, if that's possible and makes sense. Be wise and discerning.

Assure the group that you will help them find another leader and that you will be with them during this transition.

Note: It may not make sense to place this person in a leadership role again, depending on the reasons for removal. Your pastoral leadership will make that decision.

Share Your Thoughts

With the Author: Your comments will be forwarded to the author when you send them to *zauthor@zondervan.com*.

With Zondervan: Submit your review of this book by writing to *zreview@zondervan.com*.

Free Online Resources at
www.zondervan.com

Zondervan AuthorTracker: Be notified whenever your favorite authors publish new books, go on tour, or post an update about what's happening in their lives at www.zondervan.com/authortracker.

Daily Bible Verses and Devotions: Enrich your life with daily Bible verses or devotions that help you start every morning focused on God. Visit www.zondervan.com/newsletters.

Free Email Publications: Sign up for newsletters on Christian living, academic resources, church ministry, fiction, children's resources, and more. Visit www.zondervan.com/newsletters.

Zondervan Bible Search: Find and compare Bible passages in a variety of translations at www.zondervanbiblesearch.com.

Other Benefits: Register to receive online benefits like coupons and special offers, or to participate in research.

ZONDERVAN®

ZONDERVAN.com/
AUTHORTRACKER
follow your favorite authors